Adaptability Through Dynamic Capabilities

Herbert Endres

Adaptability Through Dynamic Capabilities

How Management Can Recognize Opportunities and Threats

Springer Gabler

Herbert Endres
Regensburg, Germany

Dissertation Universität Regensburg 2015

ISBN 978-3-658-20156-2 ISBN 978-3-658-20157-9 (eBook)
https://doi.org/10.1007/978-3-658-20157-9

Library of Congress Control Number: 2017959555

Springer Gabler

Printed on acid-free paper

This Springer Gabler imprint is published by Springer Nature
The registered company is Springer Fachmedien Wiesbaden GmbH
The registered company address is: Abraham-Lincoln-Str. 46, 65189 Wiesbaden, Germany

Acknowledgements

I would like to thank Prof. Dr. Roland Helm for providing very valuable, constructive, and profound contributions during my research project. I would also like to express my thanks to Prof. Dr. Michael Dowling for his valuable feedback on my study. Further, I am particularly grateful to my wife Sandra, my parents Maria and Wolfgang, my brother Bernhard, and my friend Michael who gave me the solid support and encouragement to accomplish my goals, believe in myself, and keep on going.

Table of Contents

List of Figures

List of Tables

List of Acronyms

AGFI	Adjusted Goodness-of-fit Index
CFI	Comparative Fit Index
DC	Dynamic Capability
DCV	Dynamic Capabilities View
d.f.	Degrees of Freedom
GFI	Goodness-of-fit Index
n.s.	not significant
PLS	Partial Least Square
RBV	Resource-Based View
RMSEA	Root Mean Square Error of Approximation
SRMR	Standardized Root Mean Square Residual

1 Introduction

1.1 The Challenge of the Fast-Changing Environment

The economic, social, and technological environment in which organizations operate today is becoming more and more dynamic and complex. This means that managers are confronted with new challenges (Barreto, 2010; Oreja-Rodríguez & Yanes-Estévez, 2010). The markets are changing at an increasing speed, and companies are faced with increasing pressure of competition, and also an increasing need for information in almost all areas. The faster development of new technologies, the increasing speed and diffusion of innovation, which manifests in shorter and shorter product life cycles, as well as the constant changes in customer needs, and the changing competitive situation, caused by the development of new economic regions like China, for instance, is leading to a rapid increase in environmental information, which makes it more and more important for companies to gather, and interpret this information in order to be able to survive in the market (Jennings & Jones, 1999; Nastanski, 2004; Barreto, 2010; D'Aveni, Dagnino, & Smith, 2010). In addition, there are numerous change processes in social, political, or legal areas taking place which have a strong influence on the development of companies (Jennings & Jones, 1999). This rapid change also implies risk and instability, which many CEOs have trouble dealing with. Reeves and Daimler (2011: 136) point out that "since 1980 the volatility of business operating margins has more than doubled, as has the size of the gap between winners (companies with high operating margins) and losers (those with low ones)." They also suggest that "market leadership is even more precarious. The percentage of companies falling out of the top three rankings in their industry increased from 2% in 1960 to 14% in 2008" (Reeves & Daimler, 2011: 136). This manifestation of a constantly changing business environment raises the question of which processes, methods, and capabilities companies possess to be able to recognize relevant events and environmental developments in time in order to hold or gain a sustainable competitive advantage over time and ensure their survival.

1.2 The Relevance of the Dynamic Capabilities Framework

Some authors have studied the appearance of Schumpeterian hypercompetition, which implies that the increasing dynamism of the markets makes it difficult to maintain a competitive position (McNamara, Valler, & Devers, 2003; Wiggins & Ruefli, 2005). Wiggins and Ruefli (2005), for instance, found that the average time span for which companies are able to sustain their competitive advantage has decreased over time. Many once successful firms were found to struggle or fail as their environments changed because they were unable to adapt to these changes successfully (Harreld, O'Reilly III, & Tushman, 2007). More than ever before, companies today need to know how to handle their resources in order to exploit opportunities or neutralize threats that arise from changes in their competitive environment (Hansen, Perry, & Reese, 2004; Kor & Leblebici, 2005; Lavie, 2006). Resources and competences have to be flexible and should be regarded more as "events" than "assets" (Von Krogh & Roos, 1996), which would in turn make renewability and evolution easier to achieve (Dierickx & Cool, 1989). Consequently, the constant development of existing resources, knowledge, and competences under adequate consideration of market developments is becoming crucial for strategic renewal.

For this reason the strategic management theory has developed from the typical Resource-Based View (RBV) to a dynamic perspective, the Dynamic Capability (DC) approach. This approach focuses on capabilities which are necessary to keep up with environmental developments. Companies which are able to systematically adapt their resources and capabilities will have a better chance of generating or holding a sustainable competitive advantage than other organizations (Teece, Pisano, & Shuen, 1997). The importance of dynamic capabilities "is now amplified because the global economy has become more open and the sources of invention, innovation, and manufacturing are more diverse geographically and organizationally" (Teece, 2007: 1321).

The dynamic capabilities are defined by Teece (2007: 1320) as "a framework, which tries to give answers for handling changes in business environment", which explains "the sources of enterprise-level competitive advantage over time," and which "provides guidance to managers for avoiding the zero profit condition that results when homogeneous firms compete in perfectly competitive markets." In order to make this framework a little more tangible, Teece breaks it down into the capabilities (1) sensing (of opportunities and threats), (2) seizing (of opportunities), and (3) managing threats and reconfiguration (of assets and organizational structures). This framework will be further developed within this dissertation and will be explained in more detail in Chapter 3.

1.3 Introduction to the Research Field "Sensing"

As mentioned above, research on strategic management has focused on the framework of dynamic capabilities as a central concept of sustained competitive advantage (Ambrosini & Bowman, 2009; Helfat & Peteraf, 2009; Helfat et al., 2007; Teece, 2007; Teece, Pisano, & Shuen, 1997). However, research on dynamic capabilities has not delivered very specific answers for explaining the sources of enterprise-level competitive advantage over time. Even though research in the last four years has made progress with the development of a clear and complete picture of dynamic capabilities, this concept still lacks clarity (Di Stefano, Peteraf, & Verona, 2010, 2014a, 2014b; Helfat & Winter, 2011; Li & Liu, 2014). To obtain an overview of the studies that have been done on dynamic capabilities, a table is provided in Chapter 3.2. Many empirical studies in this field tend to be tautological and vague, making it difficult to capture and measure these capabilities (Kraatz & Zajac, 2001; Danneels, 2008). Alongside Barreto (2010), and Ambrosini and Bowman (2009), who claimed that the concept of "dynamic capabilities" lacked "…a clear and adequate definition of the main construct" (Barreto, 2010: 275), and that "...these capabilities have been poorly specified" (Ambrosini & Bowman, 2009: 37), authors such as Di Stefano, Peteraf, and Verona, (2014a, 2014b), and Helfat and Winter (2011) have offered similar criticism. Researchers need to choose how to operationalize not only the aggregate construct (dynamic capability) but also the dimensions-related constructs, such as sensing (Barreto, 2010). This could be achieved through field research, which would allow researchers to address the micro-process question of how companies practice dynamic capabilities. For this purpose, a strategy-as-practice lens concerned with what companies do could be employed (Ambrosini & Bowman, 2009; Jarzabkowski, Balogun, & Seidl, 2007; Johnson, Melin, & Whittington, 2003; Pablo, Reay, Dewald, & Casebeer, 2007).

To be successful under the challenging circumstances described, the company has to react continuously to the threats and opportunities posed by a changing environment (White, Varadarajan, & Dacin, 2003). The top priority here is to recognize changes in the environment with the help of the right mechanism (Nastanski, 2004). According to Teece (2007), sensing of threats and opportunities serves as an important component for sustainable competitive advantage, since the success of companies mainly depends on the detection and development of opportunities and threats. Protogerou, Caloghirou, and Lioukas (2012: 620) also view the capability to sense environmental challenges as being "of utmost importance", as it provides the firm with a basis for making market-relevant decisions and thereby enables the company "to reconfigure certain capabilities before they become core rigidities". In line with Teece (2007) and Schreyögg and Kliesch-Eberl (2007), sensing is the ability to search for and identify opportunities and threats. The concepts of the present study, which are based on this understanding of sensing, will be introduced in the following chapter, and will be further explained in detail in Chapter 3.5.

1.4 Concepts of the Study and Main Research Questions

1.4.1 Concept of Model 1 – The Sensing Capability

In this concept, the sensing capability [1] is divided into two parts: "sensing activities" and "sensing performance". This makes it possible to investigate which sensing activities are relevant, meaning which sensing activities really have an effect on the sensing performance, which is defined as the actual sensing of opportunities and threats (Protogerou, Caloghirou, & Lioukas, 2012, Teece, 2007; Teece & Pisano, 1994). The sensing activities are further classified as "environmental sourcing", and the "environmental gathering and analysis mode". This concept, which has its roots in the concepts of Aguilar (1967), and Daft and Weick (1984), differs from earlier concepts because it integrates both the environmental sources and the way these sources are interpreted. Earlier research studies primarily focused on either the one (e.g. "Market orientation" studies by Jaworski and Kohli (1993) or Matsuno, Mentzer, and Rentz (2000)) or the other (e.g. "Scanning mode" studies by Aguilar (1967) or Flores et al. (2012)). Furthermore, by modeling the relationships between environmental activities ("environmental sourcing" and "environmental gathering and analysis mode") and the actual sensing of opportunities and threats, a complete sensing capability concept is presented for the first time.

1 In this dissertation, the term "sensing capability" stands for the "sensing" construct of the dynamic capabilities framework.

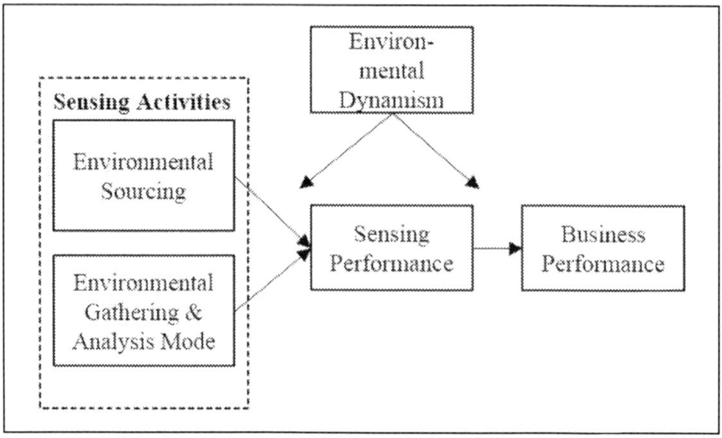

Figure 1 - Concept of Model 1 - The Sensing Capability

The investigation of this concept, which is illustrated in Figure 1, not only sheds light on the dynamic capabilities framework but also provides a comprehensive picture of the sensing capability. This specification of the sensing capability with its concrete effective activities represents a large contribution to science and management practice, as it means that management is now in a better position to handle adaptability, and generate or hold sustainable competitive advantages. To provide this contribution, the following main research question is addressed and will be answered in this dissertation:

What is the sensing capability about, meaning what kind of sensing activities lead to the actual sensing of opportunities and threats?

Impact of Environmental Dynamism on Sensing

Research (Danneels, 2008; Eisenhardt & Martin, 2000; Helfat et al., 2007; Teece, Pisano, & Shuen, 1997) also suggests the inclusion of the moderating variable environmental dynamism in studies on dynamic capabilities, because different effects have been shown under high and low environmental dynamics, and some research results are also inconsistent (Drnevich & Kriauciunas, 2011; Pavlou & El Sawy, 2006). Management research describes environmental dynamism as "the level of environmental predictability manifested in the variance in the rate of market and industry change and the level of uncertainty about forces that are beyond the control of individual businesses" (Baum & Wally, 2003: 1110). Based on this understanding, environmental dynamism has been integrated in the concept of this study (see Figure 1) in order to address the following research question:

How is the sensing capability influenced by environmental dynamism, meaning how do sensing activities differ between high and low environmental dynamism?

Impact of Sensing Performance on Business Performance

To complete the investigation of the sensing capability, it is necessary to include a link to the business performance in the model. Business performance is the financial performance of the company, meaning the development of sales, market share, and profitability. According to Eriksson's (2014) review of dynamic capabilities, two different links between dynamic capabilities and company performance are pursued in the research studies. While some studies promote an indirect link between dynamic capabilities and company performance, and argue that dynamic capabilities affect the operational capabilities[2], which in turn affect the company performance (Eisenhardt & Martin, 2000; Helfat & Peteraf, 2003; Zott, 2003), most studies still adhere to the early conceptual view (Teece, Pisano, &

2 There is neither a consistent understanding of operational capabilities and dynamic capabilities nor a consistent distinction between dynamic capabilities and operational capabilities in the research (Barreto, 2010; Eriksson, 2014). Though some researchers try to explain that dynamic capabilities are higher-order capabilities that influence operational capabilities (Collis, 1994; Winter, 2003), they fail to provide a clear and precise classification into dynamic and operational capabilities. Therefore, it is questionable whether an indirect link of dynamic capabilities to a company's outcome can really be tested via operational capabilities.

Shuen, 1997) according to which dynamic capabilities have a direct effect on organizational outcomes (García-Morales, Llorens-Montes, & Verdu-Jover, 2007; Kor & Mahoney, 2005; Wu, 2007; Zhang, 2007). As a result of these diverse findings, it is "necessary for future research to examine whether or not a direct relationship" (Eriksson, 2014: 76) exists. By complying with this need, this thesis examines the relation between the sensing performance which corresponds to the sensing outcome and the business performance. Moreover, this study thereby goes beyond prior research, which primarily investigated the whole dynamic capabilities framework and its relation to a company's performance and not a concrete dimension of this framework such as the sensing capability (Barreto, 2010; Eriksson, 2014). The potential findings might then further confirm the business relevance of the operationalization and measurement of the sensing capability concept used. This research objective is reflected in the following research question:

How is the sensing capability related to a company's business performance?

1.4.2 Concept of Model 2 – Differences between Sensing Opportunities and Sensing Threats

Because environmental changes are often ambiguous (Ford & Baucus, 1987; Pfeffer & Salancik, 1978), the way in which they are interpreted plays a significant role in the actions (Barr, 1998; Barr, Stimpert, & Huff, 1992; Dutton, Stumpf, & Wagner, 1990; Ginsberg & Venkatraman, 1992, 1995; Gioia et al., 1994; Sharma, 2000; Tripsas & Gavetti, 2000), effectiveness, and performance of an organization (Ginsberg, 1994; Thomas, Clark, & Gioia, 1993, Thomas, Gioia, & Ketchen, 1997; Lumpkin & Dess, 2006). Specifically, the perceptions of executives seem to influence the actions of their organizations, as they filter, interpret, and categorize incoming information, and make decisions based on these interpretations (Hambrick & Mason, 1984; Starbuck & Milliken, 1988; Thomas, Clark, & Gioia, 1993). However, almost no attention has been paid to the analysis of factors forming the interpretation of market information (Milliken, 1990; O'Reilly, 1982; Sutcliffe, 1997; Vandenbosch, Saatcioglu, & Fay, 2006), especially in regard to potential differences in sensing threats and sensing opportunities (Anderson & Nichols, 2007). This issue is addressed by looking at various environmental information sources and their different effects on the sensing of threats as opposed to the sensing of opportunities. These different effects are addressed in Model 2 (see Figure 2).

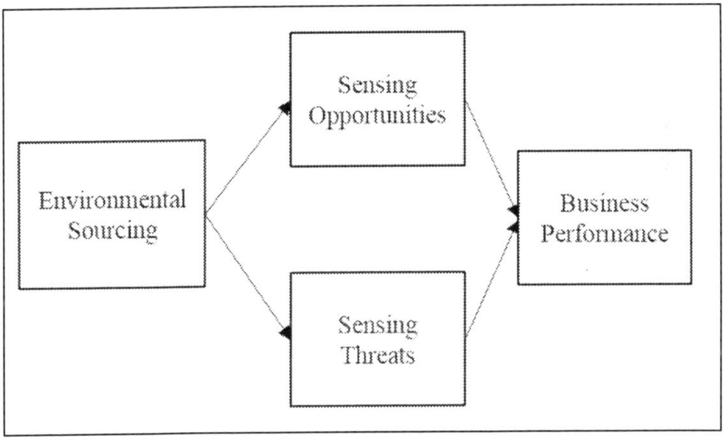

Figure 2 - Concept of Model 2 - Environmental Sourcing Differences between Sensing Opportunities and Sensing Threats

Here it can be shown how the perception of a piece of environmental information from a specific environmental source affects the interpretation of it as an opportunity or a threat. Insights derived from studying this concept will provide a guide for management to focus attention on the right environmental sourcing activities for either sensing opportunities or sensing threats depending on the circumstances and goals of the company. This provides companies with the know-how about what kind of environmental source should be used to identify opportunities and threats respectively. To sum this up, the following research question is addressed here by the investigation of Model 2:

How do environmental sourcing activities differ concerning the sensing of opportunities as opposed to the sensing of threats?

Impact of Sensing Opportunities, and Sensing Threats on Business Performance

The relation between the sensing performance and the business performance of companies of Model 1 mentioned above will also be examined for this model. However, this will occur under the changed conditions that sensing performance is divided into the two parts sensing opportunities and sensing threats. In accordance with prospect theory (Kahnemann & Tversky, 1979; Tversky & Kahnemann, 1986; White, Varadarajan, & Dacin, 2003) and threat rigidity theory (Ocasio, 1995; Staw, Sandelands, & Dutton, 1981), there might be differences in the effect of sensing opportunities on a company's business performance as opposed to sensing threats due to the different behavioral impacts on the members of a company of recognizing a threat compared to an opportunity. As far as is known, no empirical tests have been done on this. This research objective is adressed by the following question:

What is the impact of sensing opportunities on a company's business performance as opposed to the impact of sensing threats?

1.5 Structure of the Dissertation

As mentioned above, there is still no clear or concrete picture of the framework of dynamic capabilities, including the sensing capability (Ambrosini & Bowman, 2009; Barreto, 2010; Di Stefano, Peteraf, & Verona, 2010, 2014a, 2014b; Helfat & Winter, 2011; Li & Liu, 2014). In this dissertation, this issue is addressed by an investigation of the research questions outlined above. To address these questions, an empirical study was conducted based on interviews (conceptual study) and an online survey of manufacturing companies in Germany.

This dissertation is organized as follows: In Chapter 2 general frameworks and theories addressing the adaptability and sustainable competitive advantages of companies are introduced to give an overview of what concepts besides dynamic capabilities explore the survival of companies. In Chapter 3, a theoretical introduction to the models to be examined is provided, including an extensive description and theoretical foundation of dynamic capabilites, a review of the dynamic capabilities' literature, and the theoretical foundation of the sensing capability. In Chapter 4, the research hypotheses are derived. Chapter 5 gives a short introduction to the methodical basics, and illustrates the operationalization of the measurement models. Chapter 6 covers the new empirical study, starting with a description of the research design, sample selection, and survey development, and followed by the evaluation of the structural equation models, the outcome of the study, and the limitations along with future directions for research. In Chapter 7, an overall summary regarding the outcome of this dissertation is provided, as are the contributions to research and practice.

2 Frameworks and Theories around Dynamic Capabilities

2.1 Introduction to Organization and Strategic Management Theories around Dynamic Capabilities Addressing Adaptability or Sustainable Competitive Advantages

In this dynamic and complex environment as introduced in Chapter 1.1, the essence of an organization as being to coordinate people's activities and to connect these activities to a meaningful whole is challenged, as although the fast-evolving environment requires fast coordination, it nonetheless still requires efficiency within the company as well (Kieser & Ebers, 2006). This also entails the constant monitoring of the environment, and a constant questioning of how to address requests resulting from environmental changes. Since companies are developing or acquiring knowledge and resources with increasing speed, the half-life of a competitive advantage like specialized knowledge is constantly decreasing. As companies gain the specialized knowledge they require to compete, the companies which previously had a monopoly on this knowledge now lose their lead. To take the Fortune 500 companies of 1970, for example, fewer than 40% of them still existed in their original form in 1991 (Lubit, 2001). In their article, Reeves and Deimler (2011: 137) also recognize that the uncertainty "poses a tremendous challenge for strategy making", pointing out further that "traditional approaches to strategy – though often seen as the answer to change and uncertainty – actually assume a relatively stable and predictable world", and "that sustainable competitive advantage no longer arises exclusively from position, scale, and capabilities in producing or delivering an offering because all those are essentially static".

The dynamic capabilities framework addresses the above requirements regarding adaptability, and the sustaining of competitive advantage. This framework thereby fits in with other theoretical approaches aiming to explain successful adaptation and change. In strategy and organization science, and in parts of economics and decision sciences, there is still a debate concerning adapatability and sustainable competitive advantages which has not yet been resolved despite decades of research, and continues in the face of joint research efforts and the huge growth of knowledge in this area. The great amount of research and the persistence of this debate reflect the different theoretical approaches and empirical methods applied to increase knowledge in the adaptation process of companies. The nature and source of the debate are highlighted by a comparison of strategic management and organizational ecology theories. Organizational ecology theories focus on selection, variation, and retention processes to explain the evolution of populations of organizations, while strategic management theories focus on firm-level adaptation as a function of strategy and organization design. In addition, organizational ecology research, is mostly disconnected from adaptation at the level of the individual organizational unit, and is therefore often regarded as not being able to contribute directly to explaining firm-level adaptation. Moreover, according to Lewin and Volberda (1999: 519) "the weak comparability of empirical findings across strategic management studies derives from the many competing theoretical formulations, proliferation of model specifications, and the absence of shared definitions for variables and measures."

Consequently, the debate on adaptability and sustainability of companies continues. To provide an overall picture, it is deemed necessary to address the organisation theories as well as the strategic management theories. An overview of the most prominent approaches which discuss adaptability or sustainable competitive advantages will be provided in Chapter 2.2. This overview has primarily been derived from Lewin and Volberda (1999), and Kieser and Ebers (2006). By introducing the frameworks or theories and their respective critical analysis, the intention is to provide some background information on the origin of the development of the dynamic capabilities framework and the reasons behind it, along with a general understanding of the necessity of addressing adaptability and sustainable competitive advantages. Some readers might therefore also expect absorptive capacity or the knowledge-based view to be listed, but as these concepts have been not defined as a general theory of the firm, but, as regards the absorptive capacity, more as a concrete dynamic capability (Reilly & Scott, 2010; Wang & Ahmed,

2007), and, as regards the knowledge-based view, more as a supplement to a theory (Foss, 1996; Phelan & Lewin, 2000), they will not be addressed here.

2.2 *Prominent Organization Theories and Strategic Management Theories Addressing Sustainable Competitive Advantages and Adaptability*

2.2.1 *Prominent Organization Theories Addressing Adaptability*

2.2.1.1 *Behavioral Theory*

Simon (1976: IX) describes the aim of behavioral theory as intending "to show how organizations can be understood in terms of their decision processes", since "decision-making processes hold the key to the understanding of organizational phenomena" (Simon, 1976: XL). Applying this to the context of this study means that managerial decision-making is the driver for companies' ability to adapt to changes. In the context of their behavioral theory of the firm, Cyert and March (1963) were among the first to question that companies possess a perfect knowledge base, strive for profit maximization, and do not suffer from internal resource allocation problems which existed beforehand. Here, they focused on a small number of key economic decisions which were made by the firm, and then developed process-oriented models of the firm. Their theory has been applied to internal resource allocations, competitive dynamics, and predictions regarding the behavior of other organizations. According to their theory, firms thrive more by satisficing rather than maximizing goals. This is rooted in Simon's (1955) concept of bounded rationality, according to which individuals can only possess limited rationality because of the limitation of information, the cognitive limitations of their minds, and the restricted time for decisions to which everyone is exposed. Consequentially, individuals are only able to act as "satisficers" and not as "maximizers", since a lack of information renders optimal solutions or maximization impossible.

Behavioral theory was one of the first theories to claim that uncertainty, which is caused by unpredictable events in the business environment or by unpredictable consequences of companies' actions, for instance, should be included in the management decision process. Due to uncertainty avoidance, most organizations in the past have tended to focus on verified data instead of uncertain estimates in order to protect themselves, and some organizations still do so today. As a result, the company follows standard procedures and a policy of reacting instead of being proactive, and hence becomes increasingly inert. This becomes visible in short-run focused actions rather than long-run actions like the future-oriented forecasting of the environment with an integrated consciousness of uncertainty (Mahoney & Rueschemeyer, 2003). This lack of awareness was addressed by Cyert and March (1963), resulting in the emergence of a new approach of adaptability or strategy for survival. Since uncertainty will always exist, companies need to integrate this issue in their decisions, and structure, which implies a continuous process of adaptation. Here, Cyert and March (1963) suggested dividing the adaptation process into three different phases within the decision process: adaptation of goals, adaptation in attention rules, and adaptation in search rules.

Critics have deemed highly questionable the virtual assembly of the firm, with the decision-making process as the unit. There has further been loud support for profit maximization rather than for satisficing behavior within companies, which is one of the core elements of behavioral theory (Ahuja, 2007). Furthermore, the adaptation process by Cyert and March has been criticized because it was primarily applied to a company's past experience (Mahoney & Rueschemeyer, 2003). Besides this criticism, some important aspects introduced by behavioral theory, like the consideration of uncertainty or the importance of the decision-making process, for instance, have found their way into the current literature on adaptability or handling environmental dynamics such as the dynamic capabilities framework.

2.2.1.2 *Organizational Learning Theory*

Organizational learning theory is a specific form of the behavioral decision-making theory. The work of organizational learning researchers like Peter Senge (1990) ties in with the capability-based theory, which will be described later. The assumption behind organizational learning theory (Argyris & Schön, 1978; Huber, 1991) is that organizations have some unique skills as regards learning based on past experience which allow them to align with their environment. This learning process is both reactive and proactive, and allows for the development of knowledge as well as for the association of the suitability of past actions and the potential usefulness of future actions. Under these conditions, companies remain vital by balancing local and expanded search in order to achieve their most important functions, and remain open to continuous reflection and monitoring at the same time in order to meet the challenges of external change and internal inertia (Lewin & Volberda, 1999).

The typical organizational learning circle is a reciprocal circle which starts with individual beliefs (about the environment or the way to solve problems, for example) influencing individual actions, and therefore also organizational actions, which again affects the environmental reactions and again, in turn, the individual beliefs. Therefore, different risks are involved, which result from the experience-based learning. This includes learning the wrong things or learning nothing because of individuals' distorted perceptions, which might be caused by their remembering the wrong things or drawing the wrong conclusions from past events or experiences. Organizations really struggle to interpret the past correctly because environmental developments are quite complex and uncertain, and often cannot be directly assigned to specific environmental events. In the case of an opaque past, individuals especially tend to interpret past experience in a way that is convenient and familiar (March, 1994). In addition to these issues, organizational learning might also fail if individuals within the organization do not communicate what they have learned, which, in turn, might be caused by fixed or constrained role structures within the company (Simon, 1991). Therefore, although the organizational learning theory has received a great deal of praise, it cannot be understood as the ultimate way to survive. However, organizational theory can serve as a rough filter in order to eliminate practices which have a very strong negative impact on company performance (Denrell, 2002, 2004). Some of these considerations from organizational learning theory can also be found in the dynamic capabilities framework, as will be shown later.

2.2.1.3 Contingency Theory

The assumption behind Contingency Theory (Burns & Stalker, 1961; Lawrence & Lorsch, 1967) is that companies have to achieve a "fit" with the conditions provided by their environment. It further assumes that there is an ideal organizational structure or design for each situation, in contrast to earlier theories, which assumed that there are no universally valid organizational principles. A more static and more flexible organizational design, for instance, would be better suited to a more stable or dynamic environment (Burns & Stalker, 1961). Furthermore, according to the contingency theory, the company size, the business model, or the manufacturing method also play a relevant role in assessing the organizational structure (Kieser & Ebers, 2006).

Accordingly, by using the contingency theory of the firm, adaptability would be set equal to organizational adaptation, which refers to the ability of managers to adapt the organizational design or structure appropriately to the situation, that is, the external conditions and the company's current situation (Lewin & Volberda, 1999). The emphasis in the contingency theory of the firm lies primarily on the reactive adaptation to circumstances rather than on the proactive handling or influencing of the environment, which, by contrast, is part of the dynamic capabilities framework.

2.2.1.4 *Strategic Choice Theory*

As opposed to the contingency theory, the strategic choice or managerial choice perspective (Child, 1972, 1997; Miles & Snow, 1994) argues that organizations are not just reactive recipients of environmental influence but also have the power and opportunity to shape the environment. According to claims by Hrebiniak and Joyce (1985), or Mintzberg (1979), or many other proponents of the strategic choice approach, adaptation is a dynamic process that is subject to both environmental forces and managerial action. Strategic choice theories for firm strategy imply that management should consider the many ways in which an organization interacts with its environment through the process of reciprocal adaptation between the organization and its environmental domain (Lewin & Volberda, 1999). This idea will be found again in the concept of dynamic capabilities.

2.2.1.5 *Population Ecology Theory*

Along with evolutionary management theory, population ecology theory (Hannan & Freeman, 1977) is one of the two most common forms of the evolutionary theory of the firm in the management literature. Population ecology theory is especially used to explain companies' processes of adjustments, with the central idea being that the environment drives the selection of organizations. This selection happens through competition and resource scarcity. In this concept the intention or the action of the management has almost no impact on adaptation (Lewin & Volberda, 1999). This selection process is analyzed at the population level of organizations, as the object of interest is the distribution of fitness across the population of organizations rather than the fitness of any individual organization. Moreover, organizational attempts at restructuring and transformation are seen as being useless, and as even reducing a company's chances of survival. A firm's inability to adapt is a direct outcome of structural inertia. Like the concept of fitness, that of structural inertia refers to a fit between the adaptive behavioral capabilities of organizations and their particular environments (Hannan & Freeman, 1984). According to the population ecology theory, "organizations accumulate structural and procedural baggage as a result of retention processes" (Lewin & Volberda, 1999: 520), and their ability to respond to changes in their environment directly causes the build-up of structural inertia. In population ecology theory, companies survive according to their high reliability and specialization. However, the selection of companies increases as environmental rates of change surpass firm rates of change. As regards strategy, the extreme implications from the population ecology theory are that management makes no difference and the best that companies can do is to focus on their specializiation in a niche, and hope that this works out. If one takes this theory further, if new entrants come into a market and define a new environment, the existing players in its specific market segments or niches are threatened, and after a certain time often selected out (Miller, 1990; Lewin & Volberda, 1999). This kind of fatalistic approach has not found its way into current management theories – on the contrary, companies' proactive shaping of the market has become more and more dominant in literature and management practice, as the dynamic capabilities framework shows. However, the population ecology theory makes it clear that the fitness between the environment and the organization plays a central role in survival.

2.2.1.6 Evolutionary Management Theory

According to Malik and Probst (1981), evolutionary management needs to avoid active intervention within the company. The management is hence obliged to cultivate prerequisites, and to serve as a catalyst in order to enable the development of specific desirable results and events for the company. The management does not work on rigid processes or routines but on a learning-by-doing approach, meaning that problem-solution trials are continuously driving the structure and the processes within the company. Evolutionary management means that the management is fully aware of the temporary nature of the organizational structure or processes. No clear or generalizable "how-to-do" principles are used here, and no details are determined (Probst, 1987). It is more about building a context or framework which allows the structure, relationships, or system to find their own shape

(Probst, 1987). Consequently, evolutionary management theory is more concerned with the right attitude than the right processes, guidelines, or routines. This leads to a very high flexibility of companies. In contrast to the contingency approach, evolutionary management cannot destroy the adaptability of the company but instead reflects a high adaptability because it destroys or avoids complexity, and misuses the system (Malik & Probst, 1981). However, although this destruction or avoidance of complexity and principles might lead to a high adaptability, it does not necessarily lead to good company performance. Aspects like efficiency or effectiveness do not feature at all in this theory, which makes it hard for a company to survive, especially in today's highly competitive environment. This makes clear that adaptability does not just mean flexibility, because a company that is flexible but unable to make a profit over time will fail sooner or later (Kieser & Ebers, 2006).

2.2.1.7 *Institutional Theory*

The potential of institutional theory to explain adaptation is illustrated by Greenwood and Hinings (1996). One fundamental reason why organizations resist change is that they are embedded in their institutional context. But what does institutional context mean?

According to institutional theorists, regularized organizational behaviors are the product of ideas, values, and beliefs that originate in the institutional context (Meyer & Rowan, 1977; Meyer, Scott, & Deal, 1983). Organizations must take care of institutional expectations to survive, even though these expectations may have little to do with the idea of performance accomplishment (D'Aunno, Sutton, & Price, 1991; Scott, 1987). Here, Greenwood and Hinings (1996) quote the example of an accounting firm which is organized as a professional partnership because that form is defined as the right way of organizing an accounting company (institutional pressure), and not because it is the most effective or efficient way of managing the tasks. This example makes it quite clear that based on the institutional theory, an organization not only has to respond to market forces but also to institutional pressures or demands, such as regulatory agency requirements, or general social expectations (Greenwood & Hinings, 1996). Hence, seeing adaptability from the standpoint of institutional theory would mean that the higher the structured institutional context was, the higher an organization's resistance to change would be. Applying this to the strategy of a company, institutional theories imply that adaptation and survival are achieved by staying in alignment with changing industry norms and shared logics. Firms should therefore adopt a fast follower strategy, which is assumed to be directly connected to long-term survival (Lewin & Volberda, 1999). Following this theory would therefore also imply that companies were more driven by the environment, or in this context, the institutional context, than driving the development of the environment themselves, and the survival of companies depends on their capability to adapt to institutional contexts.

After this provided overview of the organization theories, the following chapter will present the prominent strategic management theories addressing sustainable competitive advantages and adaptability, before the conclusion from all the presented frameworks and theories is given in Chapter 2.3.

2.2.2 Prominent Strategic Management Theories Addressing Sustainable Competitive Advantages and Adaptability

2.2.2.1 Porter's Market-Oriented Model

According to Porter's (1980) five forces model, firms can sustain competitive advantage by the industries they select and by the way they position themselves within an industry. Specifically, Porter suggests that companies position themselves in industries with weak suppliers and buyers, high entry barriers, few threats from substitutes, and limited rivalry. The forces of entry barriers, supplier power, buyer power, threat from substitutes and rivalry influence and form the attractiveness of the market (Porter, 1980). According to Porter, this framework is intended to be the basis for deriving a company's strategy and competitive positioning in order to gain or hold competitive advantages within the industry. The competitive forces approach suggests that competitive advantage stems from valuable positioning within an industry, and also from the protection of this valuable position against new entrants and competitors (Porter, 1980, 1985).

Though the five forces model allows companies to estimate and identify opportunities and threats, because of its static and structural view, it can only be a snapshot of the current environment (Teece, 2007; D'Aveni, Dagnino, & Smith, 2010). How does the assessment of rivalry or buyer power work under conditions of change, especially when boundaries between industries might be blurred? D'Aveni, Dagnino, and Smith (2010) therefore provide the example of the U.S. cell phone industry, where firms like AT&T, Apple, or Google changed their business models in 2010, which begs the question of whether these companies should now be regarded as buyers, suppliers, or rivals? Especially in this fast-changing industry we have to ask ourselves how industry boundaries and structure are to be seen. To conclude, therefore, Porter's five forces model can be used to analyze a company's current environment, anticipate how this environment will evolve based on the current situation, and then derive a company's strategy, competitive advantage, and choice as to where to position itself. However, if there are strong and constant changes, a static assessment will not be of much help. It therefore says little about how to adapt the positioning or adapt to the competitive environment, which will be addressed in regard to the dynamic capabilities framework.

2.2.2.2 Resource-Based View

Resource-based concepts have been used to explain performance differences and competitive advantages of companies since 1970 (Rubin, 1973; Wernerfelt, 1984; Prahalad & Hamel, 1990; Barney, 1991). In contrast to the market-oriented approach of Porter, this concept considers internal resources to be a central aspect of a company's planning and strategic thinking. The resource-based view focuses on the exploitation of firm-specific assets, and regards firms as a collection of resources (Penrose, 1959). While the focus of the resource-based view has mostly been clear, there have been different standpoints concerning the understanding of what resources mean and how they should be categorized.

While Wernerfeldt (1984: 172) classifed resources as "tangible and intangible assets which are tied semipermanently to the firm", Barney used the resource categories "human", "physical", and "organizational" (Barney, 1991), and Penrose categorized the resources as "tangible" or "human" (Penrose, 2009). Penrose strongly influenced the understanding of resources within the resource-based view, and broadened the understanding of resources by defining resources as a collection of different functions. Penrose (2009: 22) further points out that "it is never resources themselves that are the 'inputs' in the production process, but only the services that the resources can render. ... The services yielded by resources are a function of the way in which they are used – exactly the same resource when used for different purposes or in different ways and in combination with different types or amounts of other resources provides a different service or set of services. The important distinction between resources and services is not their relative durability, rather it lies in the fact that resources consist of a bundle of potential services and can, for the most part, be defined independently of their use, while services cannot be so defined, the very word 'service' implying a function, an activity." These considerations of Penrose, that resources should be regarded more as a source of functions or services than just as an asset, already show the first signs or maybe even the starting-point of the capability-based theory of the firm, which will be described in the next chapter, and which is fundamental to the dynamic capabilities framework.

Based on this understanding of resources, in his article on firm resources and sustained competitive advantage in 1991, Barney laid the foundations for the resource-based view of the company: namely that resources, which can either be acquired or developed, need to be valuable, rare, imperfectly imitable, and non-substitutable in order to have the potential to build a firm's sustainable competitive advantage. Barney derived this insight from his assumptions that (1) companies within an industry are heterogeneous concerning the resources they control, and (2) these resources might not be completely mobile across firms (Barney, 1991).

Barney (1991: 102) goes on to say that based on these assumptions "… value creating strategy is not simultaneously being implemented by any current or potential competitors and when these other firms are unable to duplicate the benefits of this strategy" a sustainable competitive advantage can be achieved.

There is a tremendous research stream based on the resource-based view described above, whereby researchers have tried to identify resources which enable companies to gain or hold competitive advantages over time. Importantly, there have been a number of studies that connect the resource-oriented actions and responses in regard to organizational performance, and confirm that a resource portfolio consisting of valuable, rare, imperfectly imitable, and nonsubstitutable resources leads to good company performance (Derfus et al., 2008; Young, Smith, & Grimm, 1996). However, what applies under this concept if there are dramatic changes in resource value, uniqueness, and imitability, for instance if innovations lead to a constant disruption of current resources?

Various strategy researchers (D'Aveni, 1994; Eisenhardt & Martin, 2000) argue that in today's highly dynamic environments it is difficult, if not impossible, to achieve and sustain competitive advantage at the organizational level by using resources. It is easy to imitate or replace technological resources in many high tech industries, for example. Furthermore, resources are often rapidly diffused throughout an industry (Brown & Eisenhardt, 1998). Due to the fact that resources are copied, substituted, or made obsolete quickly, the only advantages which a company can look forward to are a series of temporary ones, as existing resources lose their value and new ones are required to replace the old ones (MacMillan, 1989; D'Aveni, 1994). In other words, the two fundamental assumptions of the resource-based view according to Barney (1991), namely (1) the heterogeneity of resources across firms, and (2) the imperfect mobility of resources, are certainly questionable. Taking a look at the loss of value, inimitability, nontradability, nonsubstitutability, or rarity of a resource, for example, puts a question mark on the static resource-based theory, and renders it more of a theory of temporary advantage (D'Aveni, 1994).

Despite some criticism, the resource-based view has been and still is quite a relevant theory for explaining a company's competitive advantage, although it needs to be extended if it is still to be relevant for creating or holding sustainable competitive advantages. This has been done by developing the dynamic capability approach (Kraaijenbrink, Spender, & Groen, 2010; Lockett, Thompson, & Morgenstern, 2009).

2.2.2.3 Capability-Based Theory

On considering what is distinctive about firms in order to generate sustainable competitive advantages, we come to the conclusion that capabilities might be distinctive. Capabilities cannot be easily replicated through markets (Teece, 1986; Kogut & Zander, 1992), since the distinctiveness of internal organizations is hard to copy. This also means that entrepreneurs are not able to simply imitate the unique organizational skills just by entering a market and assembling parts, since replication cannot be done overnight, especially the replication of best practice skills. According to Nelson and Winter (1982), capabilities show their true potential in the manifestation of competencies, which reflect developed capabilities with a specific purpose for business. So, an organization's capabilities cannot be understood just as a few items on a balance sheet, but more as "organizational structures and managerial processes which support productivity" (Teece & Pisano, 1994: 540). To sum this up, the capability-based view regards the company with its structure and boundaries as a conglomerate of individual and team capabilities, which are maintained and supported by that company. The first ideas of this view go way back to Adam Smith and Karl Marx, who saw an important role in the management and division of labor concerning the developments of skills, and providing a key competence for the company. The capability paradigm has found many followers, and became quite prominent in the literature on corporate strategy during the late 1980s and early 1990s (Pettigrew & Whipp, 1991; Prahalad & Hamel, 1990; Winter, 1987). According to Hodgson (1998), the key features of the typical capability-based approach are:

(1) the emphasis on learning and growth, meaning that individuals themselves are always in a process of development and learning,

(2) the recognition of the role of radical uncertainty toward the information and knowledge within the company, and

(3) the acknowledgement of tacit knowledge within the company.

Looking at these aspects, one could come to the conclusion that in a capability-based perspective the company is more than just its cost and revenue curves, and should be understood as a form of organizing knowledge. As Teece and Pisano (1994: 552) put it, "Because of imperfect factor markets, or more precisely the non-tradability of "soft" assets like values, culture, and organizational experience, these capabilities generally cannot be bought – they must be built. This may take years – possibly decades." Accordingly, strategic emphasis is put on learning and the growth of knowledge within the firm, and this might become "the most sustainable competitive advantage" (Stata, 1989: 64).

In contrast to Porter's competitive strategy (1980), the orientation of the capability-based view is less on market evaluations and advantageous cost-revenue combinations and more on building up organizational routines and resources within the company.

According to Rumelt (1974), Teece and Pisano (1994), and Teece et al. (1994), capabilities have to be built and cannot just be bought. Teece and Pisano (1994: 552) further criticize the fact that the "capabilities approach accordingly sees definite limits on strategic options, at least in the short run. Competitive success occurs in part because of processes and structures already established and experience obtained in earlier periods." Seeing these dangers in the capability-based approach, Teece and Pisano (1994) propose the "dynamic capabilities" framework which will be explained in detail in Chapter 3.2.

2.3 *Conclusion from the Frameworks and Theories Presented*

Therefore, as described in Chapter 2.2, it is not the capability to earn a living in the here and now but the capabilities which enable the company to create new resources and to renew existing capabilities and resources which are the source of sustainable competitive advantages and thereby adaptability over time (Danneels, 2002; Winter, 2003). To hold or create these advantages, companies need to be good at learning how to do new things instead of doing specific tasks (Danneels, 2002; Reeves & Deimler, 2011), because the typically well-known competitive advantages like specialized knowledge or company-owned technologies can only exist for a transient period. While Porter's market-oriented approach and the resource-based view still has its relevance, especially in gaining and explaining temporary competitive advantages, the capability-based approach has more a long-term perspective. In regard to the organization theories it can be concluded that some ideas from these theories are taken for granted nowadays, and are also integrated within the strategic management approaches, while some are obviously wrong. Cyert and March's (1963) imperfect knowledge base and Simon's (1955) concept of bounded rationality are good examples of considerations which are taken for granted nowadays. Due to the development, examination, and discussion of the above theories, these considerations evolved, as did the minds of researchers, and were integrated in the dynamic capabilities approach. This means that earlier thoughts were included and criticism of some earlier theories, such as the issue of the reciprocal approach of the organizational learning theory, meaning that old experiences shape new actions, was addressed. The dynamic capabilities framework finally aims at building sustainable competitive advantages to adapt the company's resources and capabilities to environmental changes where customer needs, competitors' actions, or technological developments constantly evolve. More details on the background, development, and composition of this framework are provided in Chapter 3.1 and 3.2 and below to offer a basic framework and a deeper understanding before the description of the sensing dimension begins in Chapter 3.3.

3 Theoretical Introduction to the Models

3.1 Literature Review on Dynamic Capabilities

The research gap of making "dynamic capabilities more tangible by examining and specifying the sensing capability", as introduced in Chapter 1, has been derived not only from suggestions by specific researchers but also from a literature review. It is probably evident that an overview of what has been done in the research on dynamic capabilities must be gained to ensure the relevance of this research project. The two articles by Barreto (2010), and Eriksson (2014) provide a good source in this regard. In order to ensure that no important study on the topic of dynamic capabilities has been left out, a separate literature review based on the search for the keyword "dynamic capabilities" in the EBSCO Business Source Premier Database, ScienceDirect, and Google Scholar was conducted.

Table 1 below provides the outcome of this review combined with that of Barreto (2010), and Eriksson (2014), sorted by the year published descending from the earliest to the latest publication.

Study	Type of Study	Research Focus	Findings
Yi, He, Ndofor, & Wie (2015)	Empirical	DCs, speed of strategic change & per-formance	- DCs facilitate rapid strategic change - Faster implementation of strategic change leads to positive effects on per-formance; a too quick implementation causes negative performance repercus-sions - Companies need corresponding capa-bilities to enable a rapid strategic change
Von den Driesch, da Costa, Flat-ten, & Brettel (2015)	Empirical	Influencing factors on DCs	- Inverted U-shaped relationship between CEO age and DC - Positive impact of CEO tenure, core self-evaluation, and solidarity on DCs

Study	Type of Study	Research Focus	Findings
Wilden & Gudergan (2015)	Empirical	DCs and marketing/technological capabilities	- Frequent sensing and recon-figuring have stronger positive effects in environments with high competitor turbulence - Marketing capabilities are positively associated with company performance in highly competitive environments, while technological capabilities are positively associated with this in stable competitive environments
Townsend & Busenitz (2015)	Empirical	Role of DCs	- DCs are more than just sub-stantive capabilities contextualized in dynamic markets - Limited support for the argument that the dynamic capabilities of a management team enable the firm to raise more early-stage capital
Bingham, Heimeriks, Schijven, & Gates (2015)	Empirical	Multiple DCs	- Emergent theoretical framework about the development of multiple dynamic capabilities ("concurrent learning")
Lin & Wu (2014)	Empirical	Role of DCs	- DCs can mediate firms valuable, rare, inimitable, non-substitutable resources - Dynamic learning capability most effectively mediates influence of VRIN resources on performance
Eriksson (2014)	Conceptual	Processes, antecedents, and consequences regarding DCs	- Literature covers a continuum of conceptualisations of DCs from very specific to a generic set of knowledge-related processes - Antecedents of DCs are internal or external to the firm - Mechanisms by which DCs lead to firm performance outcomes are still an unresolved issue

Study	Type of Study	Research Focus	Findings
Schilke (2014)	Empirical	Second-order DCs	- Performance effect of second-order DCs is indirect and mediated by first-order DCs - Negative interaction between first- and second-order DCs
Krzakiewicz & Cyfert (2014)	Conceptual	Concept	- There is a need for a synthesis of the economic and behavioral aspects of company operations in the process of analyzing knowledge-management-related problems
Di Stefano, Peteraf, & Verona (2014a)	Conceptual	Theoretical model	- The "organizational drivetrain" as a new way of explaining and understanding dynamic capabilities
Li & Liu (2014)	Empirical	Relationship between DCs and competitive advantage	- DCs have a significant positive effect on competitive advantage - Environmental dynamism is a driver
Helfat & Peteraf (2014)	Conceptual	Influencing factors	- Introduction of the "managerial cognitive capability" concept - Specific types of cognitive capabilities underpin dynamic managerial capabilities for sensing, seizing, and reconfiguring
Kriz, Voola, & Yuksel (2014)	Empirical	Sustainability	- As markets become increasingly hyper-competitive, the dynamic capability of ambidexterity may need to be adopted as a temporary rather than a sustainable source of advantage
Wilden, Gudergan, Nielsen, & Lings (2013)	Empirical	DCs and firm performance	- Performance effects of dynamic capabilities are contingent on the competitive intensity faced by firms

Study	Type of Study	Research Focus	Findings
Schilke (2013)	Empirical	Relationship between DCs and competitive advantage	- DCs are more strongly associated with competitive advantage in moderately dynamic environments than in stable or highly dynamic ones
Ali, Peters, & Lettice (2012)	Empirical	Measures	- No established measure for either dynamic or substantive capabilities
Teece (2012)	Conceptual	Role of executives	- Certain DCs may be based on the skills and knowledge of executives rather than on organizational routines - In dynamically competitive companies entrepreneurial managers should play a critical role
Pavlou & El Sawy (2011)	Empirical	Measurable model of DCs	- DCs influence performance in new product development; implications for managerial decision-making in turbulent environments
Hodgkinson & Healey (2011)	Empirical	Development of DCs	- The DCs need to use the cognitive and emotional capacities of individuals and groups by including intuitive processes
Helfat & Winter (2011)	Conceptual	Dynamic and organizational capabilities	- The line between dynamic and operational capabilities is inevitably blurred
Fortune & Mitchell (2011)	Empirical	Effect of capabilities on selec-tion processes	- Managerial and functional capabilities have heterogeneous effects on selection processes within the company - Managerial capabilities have a particularly strong influence on acquisition exits by struggling firms
Helfat & Winter (2011)	Conceptual	Difference between DCs and operational capabilities	- The line between dynamic and operational (or ordinary) capabilities is inevitably blurred
Drnevich & Kriauciunas (2010)	Empirical	Contributions to relative firm performance	- Environmental dynamism positively affects the contribution of DCs to relative firm performance

Study	Type of Study	Research Focus	Findings
			- Heterogeneity of a capability strengthens the contribution of DCs to relative firm performance
Barreto (2010)	Conceptual	Research streams, limitations	- A new conceptualization of dynamic capabilities as an aggregate multidimensional construct
Danneels (2010)	Empirical	Resources	- Resource cognition is a missing element in dynamic capability theory
Di Stefano, Peteraf, & Verona (2010)	Conceptual	Origin and structure of DCs	- Evidence of commonalities as well as polarizing differences in understanding across DCs' research domain
Ambrosini, Bowman, & Collier (2009)	Conceptual	Levels of DCs	- Regenerative DCs either come from inside the firm or from outside, via changes in leadership or intervention of external change agents
Ambrosini & Bowman (2009)	Conceptual	Characteristics of DCs	- Review and synthesis of literature on DCs
Augier & Teece (2009)	Conceptual	Antecedents; future research	- Future developments: employment of evolutionary and behavioral theories
Easterby-Smith, Lyles, & Peteraf (2009)	Conceptual	Evolution, debates, consequences	- Future research: more longitudinal studies; diverse industries, national contexts
Prieto, Revilla, & Rodríguez-Prado (2009)	Empirical	Contextual antecedents of DCs in product development	- A context consisting of autonomy, performance management, support and trust makes dynamic capabilities more usable for continuous product development - Dynamic capabilities shape product development competences

Study	Type of Study	Research Focus	Findings
Fang & Zou (2009)	Empirical	Marketing DCs	- Evidence for marketing DCs on international joint ventures' competitive advantages and performance - Marketing DCs are influenced by resource magnitude, complementarity, organizational culture and structure
Arend & Bromiley (2009)	Conceptual	Origin, basic concept of DCs	- Four major problems that limit the potential contribution of the DCV: (1) unclear value-added relative to existing concepts; (2) lack of coherent theoretical foundation; (3) weak empirical support; (4) unclear practical implications
Athreye, Kale, & Ramani (2009)	Empirical	Regulatory changes and DCs	- Radical regulatory changes can impact capability development similarly
Benner (2009)	Empirical	Organizational response; environmental change	- Increasing use of process management practices dampened response to new generations of digital technology; effect differed for incumbents and nonincumbents - Increasing use of process management practices over time leads to a greater negative effect on incumbents' response to the rapid technological change
Severi Bruni, & Verona (2009)	Empirical	Market knowledge, technological innovation	- Dynamic marketing capabilities can contribute to a more granular understanding of management practices and performance heterogeneity in science-based settings

Study	Type of Study	Research Focus	Findings
Chen & Jaw (2009)	Empirical	Sustainable development	- Six global dynamic capabilities as the driving forces behind the creation of new "cultural" products - Technology-based firm-specific advantages help "cultural" organizations globalize their business and create value
Ellonen, Wikström, & Jantunen (2009)	Empirical	DCs and innovation	- Companies that had relatively strong dynamic capabilities in all three areas (sensing, seizing, and reconfiguration) seem to produce niche creation and revolutionary type innovations - Firms with weaker DCs produce more radical innovations
Liao, Kickul, & Ma (2009)	Empirical	DCs and innovation	- A firm's resource stock and integrative capabilities affect the innovation performance of a company - Relationship between resource stock and innovation is mediated by integrative capabilities
Macher & Mowery (2009)	Empirical	DCs and innovation	- Empirical analysis relates differences in new process development and introduction performance to firm-level organizational routines employed in the management of process innovation - Deliberate, rather than passive learning is the key to the development of dynamic capabilities

Study	Type of Study	Research Focus	Findings
McKelvie & Davidsson (2009)	Empirical	Firm-based resources and DCs	- Changes in resource bases play a more influential role in the development of dynamic capabilities than the resource stock variables that were measured at an earlier stage of firm development
Narayanan, Colwell, & Douglas (2009)	Empirical	Development of DCs	- Managers undertake specific initiatives based on their own particular cognitive orientations - Senior managers play a crucial role in the development of capabilities by influencing the organization with their specific cognitive orientation
Newe & Zahra (2009)	Empirical	Management perspectives and DCs	- Firms build absorptive capacity in value networks during their product development experiences - Dynamic capabilities are guided by a proactive entrepreneurial logic, complementing the need for reactive adaptive responses in circumstances of exogenous change
Danneels (2008)	Empirical	Antecedents; characteristics of DCs	- Antecedents are: willingness to cannibalize, constructive conflict, tolerance of failure, environmental scanning and resource slack
Døving & Gooderham (2008)	Empirical	Intermediate outcomes	- Scope of related diversification is influenced by heterogeneity of human capital, internal development routines, alliances with complementary service providers
Oliver & Holzinger (2008)	Conceptual	Characteristics of DCs; intermediate outcomes	- Political strategies are influenced by dynamic political management capabilities

Study	Type of Study	Research Focus	Findings
Helfat et al. (2007)	State-of-the-art book with cases	Focus on in-depth examples of corporate dynamic capabilities	- Review and examples of DCs
Kale & Singh (2007)	Empirical	Intermediate outcomes	- Alliance learning process is positively related to a firm's overall alliance success
Moliterno & Wiersema (2007)	Empirical	Specific DCs	Two-step organizational change capability: • decisions about whether to engage in resource divestment • decisions about which resource to divest
Ng (2007)	Conceptual	Intermediate outcomes	- Strength of DCs explain unrelated diversification
Pablo, Reay, Dewald, & Casebeer (2007)	Empirical	Characteristics of DCs	- Three phases in developing a DC: identifying DCs, enabling DCs, managing ongoing tensions
Rothaermel & Hess (2007)	Empirical	Antecedents	- Antecedents to innovation are found at the individual, firm, and network levels according to the DC perspective, and they can compensate or reinforce firm-level innovation output
Schreyögg & Kliesch-Eberl (2007)	Conceptual	Characteristics of DCs	- In addition to changing the resource configuration, DC requires the separate capability 'monitoring'
Teece (2007)	Conceptual	Antecedents; characteristics of DCs	- DCs enable business enterprises to create, deploy, and protect the intangible assets
Gilbert (2006)	Empirical	Characteristics of DCs	- Competing frames of threat and opportunity shape response to discontinuous change

Study	Type of Study	Research Focus	Findings
Hahn & Doh (2006)	Methodological	-	- Bayesian approaches for future DC studies
Karim (2006)	Empirical	Antecedents	- Structural reconfiguration is affected differently by internally developed units and acquired units
Lavie (2006)	Conceptual	Reconfiguration mechanisms	- Three mechanisms of capability reconfiguration: Substitution, evolution, transformation
Marcus & Anderson (2006)	Empirical	Characteristics of DCs, intermediate outcomes	- General DCs affect firms' competence in supply chain management, and do not affect competence in environmental management
Pil & Cohen (2006)	Conceptual	Antecedents	- How modular design practices drive the development of DCs
Slater, Olson, & Hult (2006)	Empirical	Characteristics of DCs, performance outcomes	- Strategy formation capability is a DC; firms' strategic orientation moderates relationship between strategy formation capability and performance
Zahra, Sapienza, & Davidsson (2006)	Conceptual	Antecedents; characteristics of DCs; environmental factors; performance outcomes	- How DCs are related to substantive capabilities; how the relationship between DCs and substantive capabilities is moderated by organizational knowledge and skills
Zúñiga-Vicente & Vicente-Lorente (2006)	Empirical	Performance outcomes	- Strategic moves under environmental shifts positively affect organizational survival
Kor & Mahoney (2005)	Empirical	Antecedents	- Firms with history of increased resource deployments in marketing achieve superior economic firm-level performance to firms without
Song, Droge, Hanvanich, & Calantone (2005)	Empirical	Performance outcomes	- Effect of interaction between marketing and technological capabilities on performance is only significant in a highly turbulent environment

Study	Type of Study	Research Focus	Findings
Aragón-Correa & Sharma (2003)	Conceptual	Characteristics of DCs	- How characteristics of external environments influence environmental strategy and impact on competitive advantage
Benner & Tushman (2003)	Conceptual	Antecedents	- How process management affects DCs
Blyler & Coff (2003)	Conceptual	Antecedents	- Why social capital is a necessary condition for the existence of DCs
Lampel & Shamsie (2003)	Empirical	Antecedents; characteristics of DCs	- Mobilizing and transforming capabilities play an important role in assembling and transforming resource bundles into feature films
Salvato (2003)	Empirical	Characteristics of DCs	- Organizational leaders play a crucial role in guiding evolutionary processes
Winter (2003)	Conceptual	Characteristics of DCs	- Differences between DCs and other capabilities; ad hoc problem solving is an alternative to DCs
Zott (2003)	Simulation	Performance outcomes	- How DCs are linked to differential firm performance; firms with similar DCs may have a differential performance
King & Tucci (2002)	Empirical	Antecedents	- Probability of entering a new market is increased by experiences in previous markets
Lee, Lee, & Rho (2002)	Simulation	Intermediate outcomes	- Strategic groups are less likely to exist when DCs are absent
Zollo & Winter (2002)	Conceptual	Characteristics of DCs	- Three main learning mechanisms through which organizations develop DCs
Galunic & Eisenhardt (2001)	Empirical	Characteristics of DCs	- DCs consist of a few simple, often competing rules; enables highly adaptive behavior
Makadok (2001)	Conceptual	Characteristics of DCs	- Mechanisms for economic rents: resource picking, capability building

Study	Type of Study	Research Focus	Findings
Rindova & Kotha (2001)	Empirical	Antecedents	- Introduction of the concept 'continuous morphing', which describes the transformations the firms Yahoo! and Excite made in order to hold a competitive advantage on the Internet
Eisenhardt & Martin (2000)	Conceptual	Antecedents; characteristics of DCs; environmental factors, performance outcomes	- DCs are specific and identified processes; have commonalities across firms; different types of DCs depending on market dynamism; - DCs are necessary, but not sufficient conditions for competitive advantage
Rosenbloom (2000)	Empirical	Characteristics of DCs	- Central element in DCs is the role of managers
Helfat (1997)	Empirical	Antecedents	- In response to rising oil prices, firms with larger amounts of complementary physical assets and technological knowledge invested more R&D in regard to coal conversion
Teece, Pisano, & Shuen (1997)	Conceptual	Antecedents; characteristics of DCs; environmental factors; performance outcomes	- DCs framework is a new explanation of competitive advantage; address rapidly changing environments; - DCs rest on processes, positions, and paths; - DCs are idiosyncratic
Teece & Pisano (1994)	Conceptual	Introduction to DCs	- The conceptualization of DCs

Table 1 - Dynamic Capabilities Literature Review

The literature review presented in Table 1 above will be subsumed in the following to provide a basic understanding of the development of the research field dynamic capabilities, and thereby to also show potential new research directions.
The research on the dynamic capabilities framework has grown quite fast in recent years, so what do we know about dynamic capabilities right now, more than two decades after Teece and Pisano's (1994) article, and what should be addressed by future research? In most cases, this growth is associated with numerous different definitions of and ways of understanding the respective dynamic capabilities, followed by different measurements and operationalization approaches of this framework. Although some empirical studies have been conducted in this field, most of them have been qualitiative in nature because of missing measurements, or unconcrete, equivocal variables (Barreto, 2010; Eriksson, 2014). This insufficient formulation of a transparent framework with clear statements regarding the relationships among key constructs or variables, and a clear measurement, has "led to the existence of an important but less than coherent stock of work moving in different directions" (Barreto, 2010: 274).

In regard to the literature, dynamic capabilities are seen as a framework that aims at changing resources and capabilities (e.g. Helfat et al., 2007; Teece & Pisano, 1994; Winter, 2003), or at changing routines (e.g. Zahra, Sapienza, & Davidsson, 2006; Zollo & Winter, 2002). This changing purpose is addressed by DC-specific processes, the studies of which range from the very specific to a generic set of knowledge-related processes (knowledge accumulation, knowledge integration, knowledge ultilisation, knowledge transformation). Though some of these processes are specific, they differ in their terms and definitions. They are not clearly identifiable and therefore not tangible, which makes it quite hard to derive specific management implications. Future research could therefore make a major contribution by clearly exposing and determining the relevant process terms, and examining these processes in more detail to provide a more holistic understanding of parts of this framework. In addition, a clear and consistent operationalization via these generic knowledge processes would help to improve the understanding of the operating mechanisms behind the DCs.

There are some major differences found in the literature review concerning the external environments to which dynamic capabilities are ascribed. Here, research standpoints and results range from the relevance of the concept to highly dynamic environments, to different degrees of environmental dynamism, to both dynamic and stable environments. Clarifying this issue would move the research on dynamic capabilities forward (Barreto, 2010).

The outcomes of dynamic capabilities were found to be another unresolved issue in the research on this topic. In particular, the question of whether there are direct or indirect links between DCs and companies' performance outcomes is answered differently in the literature. From this perspective, it is necessary to examine and clarify this relationship by future research.

To sum up, this literature review shows that there is not much research into making dynamic capabilities more concrete or tangible in order to obtain more practical recommendations for management, or a clearer picture of what dynamic capabilities are about. As is mentioned in the introduction, the research on DCs is still "plagued by confusion around the construct itself" (Di Stefano, Peteraf, & Verona, 2014a: 307). In this dissertation, this gap will be addressed by focusing on "sensing", which, according to Teece (2007), and Protogerou, Caloghirou, and Lioukas (2012), is the most important dimension and the fundament for the other dimensions of the dynamic capabilities framework. However, before a closer look is taken at the sensing capability (Chapter 3.3), the theoretical foundations of the dynamic capabilities framework need to be explained and understood to be able to put this dimension in context correctly.

3.2 *Theoretical Foundations of the DC Framework*

What would strategic management look like if it were assessed that the key strategic management instruments no longer had value? What if industry structure is too temporary even to be called or defined as a specific structure? Most of the organizational theories described above as well as the prominent strategic management frameworks, like Porter's five forces, the resource-based view, or the capability-based perspective, are based on the idea of a relatively stable business environment, or at least a business environment which stabilises time and again, and do not directly address the constant dynamism in the environment. So what do economic models really tell us about how to deal with constant changes in market or industry conditions, and an ever-unattainable "market equilibrium"?

Some researchers, as described in Chapter 2, have tried to answer these questions, but, as we are now aware, most of them have failed. In their behavioral theory of the firm, for example, Cyert and March (1963) were among the first to mention that a persistent, but bounded environmental information flow related to the decision-making process affecting the company's outcome was necessary in order for companies to adapt and survive. In this view, firms are engaged in searching within the environment for opportunities or new challenges, and addressing them with product or service solutions. However, this approach still begs the question of whether this kind of searching is not just an accidental and unpredictable attempt to achieve temporary advantages, and does not answer the question of how companies can have sustaining competitive edge over their competitors, and develop new capabilities.

This idea of developing new capabilities or renewing existing capabilities to gain sustainable competitive advantages has its roots in Penrose (1959), Teece (1982), and Wernerfelt (1984). Later on, researchers like Iansiti and Clark (1994), or Henderson and Mitchell (1997) began to focus on how to renew competences or capabilities in order to react to developments in the business environment. This "renewability" is directly attached to the business processes, routines, and market positions of a company. Teece and Pisano (1994) are probably among the most prominent and well-known authors to address this necessity, and came up with a very striking illustration of what the capability to renew the company, and the existing organization's capabilities could look like when they introduced the "dynamic capabilities" framework. According to Teece and Pisano (1994: 538), "Well-known companies like IBM, Texas Instruments, Phillips, and others appear to have followed a 'resource-based strategy' of accumulating valuable technology assets, often guarded by an aggressive intellectual property stance. However, this strategy is often not enough to support a significant competitive advantage. Winners in the global marketplace have been firms that can demonstrate timely responsiveness and rapid and flexible product innovation, coupled with the management capability to effectively coordinate and redeploy internal and external competences. Not surprisingly, industry observers have remarked that companies can accumulate a large stock of valuable technology assets and still not have many useful capabilities." Teece and Pisano (1994: 538) further refer to the "source of competitive advantage as 'dynamic capabilities' to emphasize two key aspects which were not the main focus of attention in previous strategy perspectives. The term 'dynamic' refers to the shifting character of the environment; certain strategic responses are required when time-to-market and timing is critical, the pace of innovation accelerating, and the nature of future competition and markets difficult to determine. The term 'capabilities' emphasizes the key role of strategic management in appropriately adapting, integrating, and reconfiguring internal and external organizational skills, resources, and functional competences toward changing environment." This coherent dynamic capabilities framework is based on empirical literature and the theoretical foundations provided by Schumpeter (1934), Penrose (1959), Williamson (1975, 1985), Barney (1986), Nelson and Winter (1982), Teece (1988), and Teece et al. (1994).

In 2002, Zahra and Nielsen (2002) confirmed that effective dynamic capabilities are sources of competitive advantage. These capabilities are necessary for survival, especially in dynamic markets, and therefore all companies need to build and develop them. Further, Arend and Bromiley (2009) assess that the dynamic capabilities framework finally delivers an answer to the fundamental question of why some companies succeed in dynamic competitive environments while others fail. The dynamic capabilities framework makes sure that the company always has a relevant set of core competencies, consisting of a superior combination of capabilities and resources resulting in a competitive advantage over rivals.

In recent years, research on strategic management has focused more and more on the framework of dynamic capabilities as a central concept of sustained competitive advantage (Ambrosini & Bowman, 2009; Helfat & Peteraf, 2009; Helfat et al., 2007; Teece, 2007; Teece, Pisano, & Shuen, 1997), or in other words the explanation of "the sources of enterprise-level competitive advantage over time" (Teece, 2007: 1320). Therefore, sustainable advantages means more than just the ownership of assets that are hard to imitate: there is a need for capabilities "to continously create, extend, upgrade, protect, and keep relevant the enterprises's unique asset base" (Teece, 2007: 1319). These capabilities, which companies require to deal with environmental dynamics successfully, have been categorized by Teece (2007) as (1) sensing – a scanning, learning and interpretive ability concerning opportunities and threats, (2) seizing – the ability to address newly sensed opportunities through marketing activities, new processes or services, and (3) managing threats and reconfiguration – the ability to recombine and to reconfigure assets and organizational structures. Recent empirical research has reflected this activity-based understanding of dynamic capabilities (for instance Ettlie & Pavlou, 2006; Kindström, Kowalkowski, & Sandberg, 2012). In the same year, the "monitoring" capability was added to this framework by Schreyögg and Kliesch-Eberl (2007), serving as the control and evaluation "instance" of the other dynamic capabilities. Their classification is different from that of Teece (2007) in order to obtain a clearer differentiation between the dimensions. On this basis, Schreyögg and Kliesch-Eberl (2007) finally determine dynamic capabilities as the organizational capability of (1) sensing – the ability to make sense out of environmental changings, (2) learning – the capacity to react to any signal from the environment in a new way, (3) reconfiguring – the ability to transform a company's asset structure, and (4) monitoring – the capacity to observe, evaluate, and control the other dynamic capabilities. Though both classifications have their relevance, a differentiation between sensing and seizing in analogy to Teece (2007), and a differentation between sensing and learning in analogy to Schreyögg and Kliesch-Eberl (2007) seems to make sense, as a more tangible and differentiated framework and a much more concrete basis can hence be derived for the study of sensing. So using Teece's (2007) framework adapted to these changings along with the dimension of monitoring from Schreyögg and Kliesch-Eberl (2007), the final dimensions of the dynamic capabilities framework are (1) sensing – the ability to search for and identify opportunities and threats, (2) seizing – the ability to address newly sensed opportunities through marketing activities, new processes or services, (3) learning – the capacity to react to any signal from the environment in a new way, (4) managing threats and reconfiguration – the ability to recombine and to reconfigure assets and organizational structures, and (5) monitoring – the capacity to observe, evaluate, and control the other dynamic capabilities. It is necessary for this adapted framework to be understood in order to be able to put in the right context the sensing capability concept described and examined in the following, which is the focus of this thesis.

3.3 The Sensing Capability

3.3.1 Theoretical Foundation for the Sensing Capability Concept in this Thesis

The ability to search for and identify opportunities and threats in the business environment is a topic relevant to many management research fields (strategic management, marketing, and entrepreneurship, for example). This ability is defined as sensing. The dynamic capabilities framework merges many activities from these fields into the sensing concept. However, sensing is not just a conglomeration of activities from different research fields; it also includes the dynamic perspective on the company and its environment (Barreto, 2010; Teece, 2007). In view of this, sensing could be regarded primarily as the information gathering and interpreting activity of a business environment with the goal of identifying opportunities or threats (Barreto, 2010; Schreyögg & Kliesch-Eberl, 2007; Teece, 2007; Teece & Pisano, 1994). Being able to identify a new business opportunity, for example, means first of all knowing if a business opportunity exists. This can only happen if the company gets the information about this new business opportunity and is subsequently able to assess the importance of this information. To do this, the environmental information sources have to be tapped, and their output needs to be effectively analyzed – an issue which will be addressed and investigated in this dissertation.

According to Teece's (2007) findings, the sensing of threats and opportunities is an important component of sustainable competitive advantage, as the success of companies primarily depends on their detecting and developing threats and opportunities. Protogerou, Caloghirou, and Lioukas (2012) also see the capability to sense environmental challenges as being of the "utmost importance", as it provides the company with a basis for making market-relevant decisions, and thereby enables the firm "to reconfigure certain capabilities before they become core rigidities" (Protogerou, Caloghirou, & Lioukas, 2012: 620). Pavlou and El Sawy (2011) regard this dynamic capability as the identifying and interpreting capability of market developments. The capacity to seek and identify opportunities or threats in the business environment is a significant issue in many fields of management research (such as entrepreneurship, marketing, and strategic management).

Four progressive steps in an individual sense-making process have been identified in the literature (Daft & Weick, 1984; Huber, 1991; May, Stewart, & Sweo, 2000; Milliken, 1990; Thomas, Clark, & Gioia, 1993):

(1) noticing a problem (Kiesler & Sproull, 1982; Koppes & Billings, 1988; Milliken, 1990);

(2) gathering information (or "scanning") (Aguilar, 1967; Hambrick, 1981, 1982; Thomas, Gioia, & Ketchen, 1997);

(3) interpreting the information (Barr, 1998; Huber, 1991; Huber & Daft, 1987; Thomas, Gioia, & Ketchen, 1997);

(4) taking action (Chattopadhyay et al., 2001; Daft & Weick, 1984; Thomas, Clark, & Gioia, 1993; Anderson & Nichols, 2007).

According to Daft and Weick (1984), or Thomas, Clark, and Gioia (1993), this sense-making process can easily be transferred from an individual perspective to an organizational perspective, which is the view taken in this study. The concept of sensing applied in this study focuses on the second and third steps of this process, which is leaned upon Teece's (2007) and Schreyögg and Kliesch-Eberl's (2007) understanding of sensing, and sheds a different light on these steps by integrating the dynamic capabilities framework.

Looked at in this way, sensing could primarily be seen as the interpreting and information gathering activity of a business environment with the aim of identifying threats or opportunities (Barreto, 2010; Schreyögg & Kliesch-Eberl, 2007; Teece, 2007; Teece & Pisano, 1994). This leads to this concept of sensing, which was already introduced in Chapter 1, and which classifies the sensing activities into "environmental sourcing", and the "environmental gathering and analysis mode". A similar categorization was suggested by Aguilar (1967), and Daft and Weick (1984). The main difference from this concept (see

Figure 1 in Chapter 1) is that a distinction is made not between scanning and interpreting, but between environmental information sourcing and the method of gathering and interpreting market information. Here, more recent research findings are referred to, which suggest that sources and the method of gathering and analyzing are the crucial ingredients for an effective scanning of the environment and, in turn, an effective sensing of opportunities and threats (Maier, Rainer, & Snyder, 1997; May, Stewart, & Sweo, 2000; Thomas, Clark, & Gioia, 1993).

When sensing is examined in this study, it is drawn from different sources of market information (Foss, Lyngsie, & Zahra, 2013; Harmancioglu, Grinstein, & Goldman, 2010; Jaworski & Kohli, 1993; Matsuno, Mentzer, & Rentz, 2000; Wang, Ellinger, & Wu, 2013) on an organizational level. Finally, by combining the sources from the intelligence generation MO construct by Matsuno, Mentzer, and Rentz (2000) with the scanning and interpretation approaches from Aguilar (1967), and Daft and Weick (1984), and adapting this to fit in with the dynamic capabilities framework, this results in the sensing concept to be investigated in this study.

Differences in Sensing Concerning Environmental Dynamism

Research also suggests the inclusion of the moderating variable environmental dynamism in studies on dynamic capabilities (Danneels, 2008; Eisenhardt & Martin, 2000; Helfat et al., 2007; Teece, Pisano, & Shuen, 1997). Yet, in his analysis of successful companies from 1870 to 1960, Chandler (1990) observed that different environmental conditions require different management behaviours, which covers more than just a high-velocity environment (Eisenhardt, 1989; Judge & Miller, 1991).

Based on the dynamic capabilities concept, the environmental context is not just that of an industry but more a business "ecosystem", including all organizations, institutions, and individuals affecting the company's business (Teece, 2007). Management research describes environmental dynamism as "the level of environmental predictability manifested in the variance in the rate of market and industry change and the level of uncertainty about forces that are beyond the control of individual businesses" (Baum & Wally, 2003: 1110), which also covers more than just a high-velocity environment (Eisenhardt, 1989; Judge & Miller, 1991). Therefore, even low-growth industries might be "dynamic" on condition that the low growth rate variance is high (Baum & Wally, 2003). By applying this understanding of environmental dynamism, organizations in a highly dynamic environment need to handle a high degree of uncertainty, and are therefore confronted more with the necessity of adapting their resource base, and reacting to developments in the business environment (Eisenhardt & Martin, 2000). By contrast, companies operating in low dynamic environments only occasionally have to respond to changing environmental conditions. Nevertheless, "occasionally" does not mean that there is no need to handle environmental dynamics in low dynamic environments. Hence, the investigation of both environmental circumstances is recommended for this purpose.

While the great majority of dynamic capabilities studies tested the effects of industry dynamism, this inquiry considers all kinds of effects on the business environment, which are reflected in the aspects "technology change rate", "competition intensiveness", "product change rate", and "customer segment differentiation degree" (Baum & Wally, 2003). This approach is strongly recommended by authors such as Teece (2007), and Baum and Wally (2003), because industry borders are difficult to determine, and do not cover the whole picture of the relevant business environment.

3.3.2 Theoretical Foundation for the Differentiation between Sensing Opportunities and Sensing Threats

Because environmental changes are often ambiguous (Ford & Baucus, 1987; Pfeffer & Salancik, 1978), the way in which they are interpreted plays a significant role in the affected actions and effectiveness of an organization. Specifically, executives' perceptions seem to influence their organization's actions, as executives filter and interpret incoming information, and make decisions based on those interpretations (Hambrick & Mason, 1984; Starbuck & Milliken, 1988; Thomas, Clark, & Gioia, 1993). Executives appear to categorize environmental changes as being either threats or opportunities (Dutton & Jackson, 1987; Fredrickson, 1985; Jackson & Dutton, 1988). These categorizations may influence executives' reactions to environmental changes and, consequently, may influence organizational actions (Dutton & Jackson, 1987; Thomas, Clark, & Gioia, 1993). Many studies have been conducted concerning the effect that interpreting market changes as threats or opportunities has on both organizational actions (Barr, 1998; Barr, Stimpert, & Huff, 1992; Dutton, Stumpf, & Wagner, 1990; Ginsberg & Venkatraman, 1992, 1995; Gioia et al., 1994; Sharma, 2000; Tripsas & Gavetti, 2000) and company performance (Ginsberg, 1994; Thomas, Clark, & Gioia, 1993; Thomas, Gioia, & Ketchen, 1997; Lumpkin & Dess, 2006), but almost no attention has been paid to the analysis of factors driving or forming the interpretation of market information (Milliken, 1990; O'Reilly, 1982; Sutcliffe, 1997; Vandenbosch, Saatcioglu, & Fay, 2006), especially in regard to potential differences in sensing threats as opposed to sensing opportunities (Anderson &

Nichols, 2007). This will be done in this thesis by examining Model 2 (Anderson & Nichols, 2007).

There are several definitions of threats and opportunities to be found in the literature. Singh et al. (1999) consider opportunities to be the perception of the potential for new profit, either by founding a new venture or by significantly improving an existing one. White, Varadarajan, and Dacin (2003) suggest that an opportunity is the extent to which the management perceives a market situation to be of advantage to the company's sales and/or profit. In contrast, they define a threat as the extent to which the management perceives a situation as one where the company could suffer a sales and/or profit deficit. Threats often emerge as the consequence of adverse environmental conditions, such as scarce resources, competition, or reduced market size (Staw, Sandelands, & Dutton, 1981), whilst opportunities frequently come in the form of innovations and show themselves as new ideas or the recognition of customer needs (Wang et al., 2013).

In dynamic and complex environments it is particularly vital for firms to interpret ambiguous information in a significant way (Thomas, Clark, & Gioia, 1993). Therefore, descriptive labels are attached to these events to enable a specific and effective evaluation of the equivocal data (White, Varadarajan, & Dacin, 2003). In the matter of environmental changes, this information tends to be categorized as a threat or an opportunity (Dutton & Jackson, 1987). Barr (1998: 644) suggests that "a key component in a firm's strategic response to unfamiliar environmental events is the interpretations managers develop about the event itself". This is driven by the labeling of issues as threats or opportunities (Barr & Glynn, 2004; Jackson & Dutton, 1988; Kuvaas, 2002). Strategic issues are often interpreted using general labels such as "threat" or "opportunity". These labels represent the beliefs of top management concerning the potential effects of environmental events and trends (Edelman, 1977), and launch processes which drive an organization in a particular direction (Dutton, Fahey, & Narayanan, 1983). One example of a typical equivocal strategic issue is e-commerce. At the turn of the new century, the implications of e-commerce seemed to be complex and unclear for companies, which found it hard to determine whether e-commerce was a threat or an opportunity. Categorization theory describes the acquisition and application of labels such as "opportunity" or "threat" to words that identify cognitive categories – for sets of persons, things, situations, and issues that resemble one another (Cantor, Mischel, & Schwartz, 1982). Jackson and Dutton (1988) found that issues labeled as positive, controllable, and involving potential gain were more likely to be seen as opportunities, while those characterized as negative, uncontrollable, and involving potential loss were seen as threats (Anderson & Nichols, 2007).

While it has been shown in the literature that interpreting issues as being threats or opportunities has a significant effect on the actions and performance of companies (Dutton, Stumpf, & Wagner, 1990; Ginsberg & Venkatraman, 1992, 1995; Gioia et al., 1994; Sharma, 2000; Thomas, Clark, & Gioia, 1993), there is little research examining what information or information sourcing leads to the perception of a situation or condition as representing a threat or an opportunity. Previous research has shown that the top management's perception of a strategic issue affects the range of solutions considered in an organization (Billings, Milhurn, & Schaalman, 1980), influences the volume of resources dedicated to a particular project (Staw & Ross, 1978), and has an effect on the steps made toward organizational change (Dutton & Duncan, 1987; Dutton, Fahey, & Narayanan, 1983). Therefore, it is assumed that the way the top management interprets a strategic issue will systematically influence action at the organizational level. Once a label has been attached to a strategic issue or a major environmental event or change, the cognitive processes of key decision-makers work in this direction, which, in turn, affects organizational processes, and in some cases this could even mean a strategic shift for the company (Dutton & Jackson, 1987). In addition, the perception of the strategic issues or the environmental event and its interpretation also has a direct impact on the allocation of resources (White, Varadarajan, & Dacin, 2003).

However, what does actually influence whether information is recognized or perceived as a threat or an opportunity? The classification of environmental information depends on a variety of reasons, such as the diversity of the information gathered, the time spent searching for data (Anderson & Nichols, 2007), or the perceived controllability of a market situation (White, Varadarajan, & Dacin, 2003). Therefore, the question to ask is whether the environmental source, or the information from the environmental source, has such a characteristic, and therefore tends to have a different effect on whether it is sensed as being an opportunity or a threat. Up to now, the literature on scanning, for instance, has mostly considered environmental events to be one category (Anderson & Nichols, 2007; Thomas, Clark, & Gioia, 1993; White, Varadarajan, & Dacin, 2003). Considering the differences in perception of, interpretation of, and response behavior toward threats and opportunities mentioned above, it seems evident that the categorization of an environmental change as a threat or an opportunity might evoke a different sensing result. These assumptions are supported by many researchers, who suggest that the way in which a problematic situation is interpreted has a substantial effect on subsequent information processing, decision making, and behavior (Dutton & Duncan, 1987; Dutton & Jackson, 1987; March & Simon, 1958; Tversky & Kahneman, 1981).

What has not been forthcoming is an empirical investigation of environmental sourcing, and its varying impact on the actual sensing of threats and opportunities. There has evidently been some investigation into the perception of threats and opportunities, but there has not yet been any examination of a comparison of different environmental sourcing activities in regard to a company's sensing opportunities as opposed to threats. One aim of this study is to analyze the effects of environmental sourcing on sensing threats and sensing opportunities (Model 2). This will render more tangible the sensing capability and therefore the DCs.

4 Derivation of the Research Hypotheses

4.1 Brief Synopsis of this Study's Research Field

Now that the theoretical foundations of this study have been introduced, a short summary of the research field will be given, followed by the hypotheses in Chapter 4.2.

As mentioned in the introduction, this dissertation addresses the investigation of the abstract concept of dynamic capabilities, which needs to be broken down into concrete and manageable aspects. To achieve this, the focus is on the sensing dimension of the dynamic capabilities framework. By integrating different theoretical concepts and research results (strategic management, marketing, entrepreneurship, organizational science) under the heading of sensing, the sensing concept is operationalized and empirically examined. Hence, this is a response to numerous calls for future research emphasizing that more empirical studies should be conducted to gain a better understanding of dynamic capabilities.

By breaking down the sensing dimension into concrete, measurable activities, this study also provides clear and very concrete practical implications for management. The effects of specific environmental sources on the sensing of opportunities and threats, and the method of gathering and analyzing environmental information concerning the sensing of opportunities and threats (Model 1) are both investigated. This therefore goes beyond earlier market orientation or environmental scanning research studies, which mainly use environmental sources as parts of large constructs without examining the specific effect of each environmental source. Furthermore, the sources which were the focus of earlier studies were mainly investigated regarding their relation to the number of ideas, to innovations, or to business performance, but not in regard to their actual impact on sensing opportunities or threats.

Moreover, the great majority of studies on dynamic capabilities test the effects of industry dynamism, while this study considers the entire business environment as a moderating variable (Model 1), thereby providing a further contribution to research.

A further main issue which is addressed by this study is the research question concerning whether various environmental information sources have different effects on the sensing of threats as opposed to the sensing of opportunities (Model 2). In addition, the ambiguous research results and theories with respect to the impact of sensing threats and sensing opportunities on the business performance of companies (Chattopadhyay, Glick, & Huber, 2001) begs another question: whether it is more relevant for companies to sense threats or to sense opportunities. This issue is also addressed in this study (Model 2).

4.2 Derivation of the Research Hypotheses

As described above, the addressed research field concerning the sensing of opportunities and threats gives reason to expect that substantiating and operationalizing the sensing capability will lead to new insights for science and management practice. This approach provides a more tangible sensing capability and hence sheds light on the dynamic capability framework, which still remains abstract. Therefore, conceptual models have been set up, as was mentioned in the introduction. While Model 1 (see Figure 1) focuses on the investigation of the sensing capability as a whole by examining the impact of sensing activities on sensing performance, Model 2 (see Figure 2) investigates the differences in environmental sourcing regarding the sensing of opportunities as opposed to the sensing of threats.

Earlier research has examined and confirmed parts of the sensing activities in the form of environmental scanning activities, and their causal effects on constructs such as adaptability (e.g., Fey & Denison, 2003; Goll & Rasheed, 1997; Nadler, 1998; Senge, 1990), or market orientation (e.g., Matsuno, Mentzer, & Rentz, 2000; Narver, Slater, & MacLachlan, 2004). Since many authors, such as Barney (1995), Teece (2007), or Ginsberg and Venkatraman (1995), agree that an adaptive company is one that recognizes market trends, identifies the threats and opportunities within a market, and adjusts to new environmental conditions, the hypotheses have been derived accordingly.

The hypotheses from both models are derived and explained in the following two chapters (4.2.1 and 4.2.2).

4.2.1 Derivation of the Hypotheses of Model 1 – The Sensing Capability

The following figure provides an overview of the examined hypotheses of Model 1. The concrete derivation of these hypotheses will be described in the following sections.

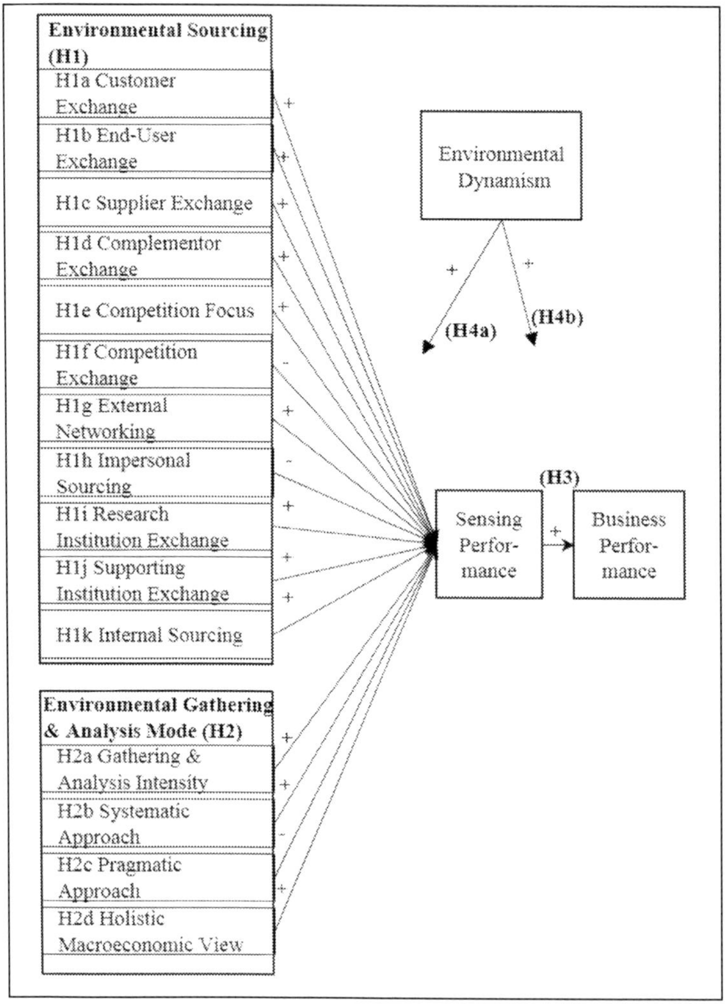

Figure 3 - Hypotheses of Model 1

4.2.1.1 Environmental Sourcing and Sensing Performance

In this study, environmental sourcing is defined as the tapping of internal and external information sources to gather relevant information about the business environment or environmental changes. Kohli, Jaworski, and Kumar (1993) already mentioned most of these sources (customer, end-user, competition, networks, media and internal research) in their MARKOR scale. Matsuno, Mentzer, and Rentz (2000) further added macroeconomic elements and suppliers as relevant sources. Both Kohli, Jaworski, and Kumar (1993) and Matsuno, Mentzer, and Rentz (2000) concluded positive causal relationships between these sources and the market orientation of a company and, as mentioned earlier, it can be derived that sensing performance effects might also be caused by these sources (Barney, 1995; Ginsberg & Venkatraman, 1995; Teece, 2007). Furthermore, the literature on dynamic capabilities brought institutions and complementors into play to capture a more complete set of the facets of environmental sourcing, as explicated by the theory (Teece, 2007).

Value Chain Partners and Sensing Performance

As Kohli, Jaworski, and Kumar (1993), and Matsuno, Mentzer, and Rentz (2000) have already found, customer exchange, end user exchange, and supplier exchange lead to a higher market orientiation. Based on this generated knowledge and the improved understanding of such value chain partners, new business opportunities or business threats, such as new customer preferences, could be identified, which indicates a higher sensing performance (Harmancioglu, Grinstein, & Goldman, 2010; Hurmelinna-Laukkanen, 2012). It is therefore expected that:

> *Hypothesis H1a. Customer exchange is positively associated with a company's sensing performance.*

> *Hypothesis H1b. End-user exchange is positively associated with a company's sensing performance.*

Hypothesis H1c. Supplier exchange is positively associated with a company's sensing performance.

Complementors and Sensing Performance

According to Teece (2007), considerably less attention has been paid to another market participant relevant to exchange: the provider of complementary goods. Since many companies are exposed to these dependencies, a regular exchange with these "partners" might be useful. Simple changes in complementary goods could instantly make related products redundant unless product adaptations are made. Furthermore, a complementary goods provider might deliver information about changes in the market. This information might help companies to identify new developments in their business environment more easily, which indicates a higher sensing performance (Teece, 2007). Hence:

Hypothesis H1d. Complementor exchange is positively associated with a company's sensing performance.

Competitors and Sensing Performance

Though the assessment of customer needs plays a central role in scanning the environment (Kohli & Jaworski, 1990), companies that are focusing too strongly on these needs might disregard competitors' actions and their effect on customer preferences (Day & Wensley, 1983). Porter also (1980) points out the importance of considering the competition to be able to anticipate competitors' actions. Since Kohli and Jaworski (1990) as well as Matsuno, Mentzer, and Rentz (2000) confirm in their research that there is a higher market orientation when competition is observed regularly, it can be assumed that this competitor orientation also leads to a higher sensing performance.

Based on the literature review in Chapter 3.1, the effect of the competition exchange needs to be included in the models of this study. Researchers' views vary as to whether there is a positive or negative relationship between competition exchange and sensing performance, because cooperation with competition carries a certain conflict potential. On the one hand, contact to the competition could enhance know-how throughout the organization, and might therefore help to identify opportunities and threats (Hurmelinna-Laukkanen, 2012; Jung-Erceg et al., 2007), but on the other hand, information about developments on the market, such as emerging new customer segments or new regulations, might lead to a competitive advantage and may result in competitors being reluctant to pass on this information. This, in turn, might lead to a protective behavior between competitors that questions the value of the information exchanged (Hurmelinna-Laukkanen, 2012). Since companies do not wish to disclose sensitive success-related information but would like to get that information from the competition, it can be assumed that companies engaging in a strong competition exchange might fail to recognize relevant market developments, and therefore decrease their sensing performance.

Following the arguments above, it can be suggested that:

> *Hypothesis H1e. Competition focus is positively associated with a company's sensing performance.*
>
> *Hypothesis H1f. Competitor exchange is negatively associated with a company's sensing performance.*

External Networking, Impersonal Sourcing, and Sensing Performance

As Hitt et al. (2001), and Helm and Gritsch (2014) observe, external network contacts could be particularly rich sources of information on the environment. The most common professional network platforms are business clubs and industry associations, which are covered by our "external network exchange" variable.

Networks create ongoing social contact and dialog which could provide the latest information on market developments (Hitt et al., 2001), and therefore increase an organization's sensing performance.

Impersonal sourcing, including media such as newspapers, trade publications and magazines, seems to be an obvious external information source used by many companies. Hills and Shrader (1998), however, found that successful entrepreneurs focus primarily on personal contacts and not on classical media usage, because personal sources provide richer information than written sources (Daft & Lengel, 1986; Holland, Stead & Leibrock, 1976). Based on this, one could derive that media sourcing does not deliver much valuable information concerning opportunities or threats in the business environment, and might therefore even be detrimental to a company's sensing performance.

In line with the reasons mentioned above, it might be concluded that:

Hypothesis H1g. External networking is positively associated with a company's sensing performance.

Hypothesis H1h. Impersonal sourcing is negatively associated with a company's sensing performance.

Institutions and Sensing Performance

Clusters such as the Silicon Valley Cluster illustrate how effective collaboration between research institutions and the surrounding companies works. These days, it is not only the IT companies which have discovered the value of institutional relationships but also other industries, such as the automobile industry. The great majority of institutional cooperations are made with universities. These relationships represent a knowledge source for small and large companies (Dowling & Helm, 2006; Jung-Erceg et al., 2007; Lorenzoni & Lipparini, 1999). In contrast to competitors or suppliers, universities tend to share their knowledge because of the scientific ethos of their experts. Since there is no need to feel skeptical about a potential important information loss because of competitive advantages, companies and universities make more of an effort to participate actively in such partnerships (Fey & Birkinshaw, 2005; Möller & Rajala, 2007). The above reasons demonstrate that the exchange with research institutions could bring a competitive edge due to a noticeable lead in knowledge. Ellonen, Wikström, and Jantunen (2009) note in their qualitative study that companies that work closely with universities show a good sensing performance.

According to Teece (2007), supporting institutional structures have a major impact on the market since they may support innovation, and thereby influence the competition. Further, the knowledge and assets of supporting institutions (e.g. a country's development institutions, state-owned promotional institutes, funding establishments) could be integrated into new value-added combinations, and thereby shape the market (Teece, 2007). Therefore, supporting institutions might play a relevant role in market analysis and in discovering opportunities or threats.

Based on these arguments, it is assumed that:

Hypothesis H1i. Research institution exchange is positively associated with a company's sensing performance.

Hypothesis H1j. Supporting institution exchange is positively associated with a company's sensing performance.

Internal Sourcing and Sensing Performance

People within the company could be valuable information sources in the business environment. Particular individuals who are in direct contact with external constituents, such as purchasing managers, public relations directors, or customer service employees, may be relevant for this purpose (Rosenkopf & Nerkar, 2001). Matsuno, Mentzer, and Rentz (2000) also attach great importance to internal sources for keeping track of external developments, which might also drive a company's sensing performance. Hence:

Hypothesis H1k. Internal sourcing is positively associated with a company's sensing performance.

4.2.1.2 Environmental Gathering & Analysis Mode and Sensing Performance

Environmental information needs to be gathered and then analyzed to sense specific changes in the environment (Teece, 2007; Thomas, Clark, & Gioia, 1993). Information gathering is thereby defined as "the process through which an organization obtains information from internal and external sources" and information interpretation is "the process through which organizations make sense of new information that they have acquired" (Flores et al., 2012: 643).

The Intensity, Systematic Approach, and Pragmatic Approach of Gathering and Analyzing, and Sensing Performance

In gathering and interpreting upcoming external events or developments, individuals within a company do not have much leeway when analyzing the information. According to Daft and Weick (1984), these activities are aggregated in an organizational method of gathering and analyzing environmental information because an organization's culture, structure, and processes do not leave much room for individual actions (Daft & Weick, 1984). By acknowledging the relevance of gathering and analyzing environmental information, companies need to raise the question of how to do so. Diverse authors differentiate these activities with the success factors of "intensity" (Aguilar, 1967; Anderson & Nichols, 2007; Daft, Sormunen, & Parks, 1988; Farh, Hoffman, & Hegarty, 1984) and "systematics" (Aguilar, 1967; Fahey & King, 1977; Helm, Krinner, & Schmalfuß, 2014). Applying the success factor of "intensity" to the field of this study would imply that the more time is spent on gathering and analyzing market information, the more opportunities and threats are identified, which means a higher sensing performance. In accordance with the findings from Helm, Krinner, and Schmalfuß (2014), or authors like Aguilar (1967), and Fahey and King (1977), a systematic method of gathering and analyzing environmental information might also help to identify important developments in the market, and thereby have a positive impact on the sensing of opportunities and threats. The systematic method is hereby determined as a continuous and structured process of gathering and analyzing market information (Aguilar, 1967).

Next to these two levers for scanning the market, the 10 interviews with the top managers of 10 different companies, which were led as a pre-study to this study, revealed another approach, the pragmatic approach. All 10 top managers interviewed understood under the pragmatic approach to be a practical, solution-oriented, and straightforward way of collecting and interpreting information on developments in the market. Since there were no findings in the research in regard to the pragmatic approach, the hypothesis below is derived from the reasoning and experience of the top managers. They state that the pragmatic approach inhibits companies in their successful sensing of opportunities and threats, as a practical and straightforward collection and interpretation of market data might be too narrowly focused, and thereby opportunities or threats which do not seem to be directly related to a company's business at first glance might be overlooked.

Summing up the arguments above, the following hypotheses can be derived:

> *Hypothesis H2a. The intensity of gathering and analyzing environmental information is positively associated with a company's sensing performance.*
>
> *Hypothesis H2b. The systematic method of gathering and analyzing environmental information is positively associated with a company's sensing performance.*
>
> *Hypothesis H2c. The pragmatic method of gathering and analyzing environmental information is negatively associated with a company's sensing performance.*

Holistic Macroeconomic View and Sensing Performance

Matsuno, Mentzer, and Rentz (2000) claim that the MARKOR scale by Kohli, Jaworski, and Kumar (1993) needs to be extended with macroeconomic elements such as social and cultural trends or new regulatories. According to them, these elements are relevant drivers in the market, and observing them provides companies with a more holistic picture of the environment. Therefore, the consideration of macroeconomic changings, which is reflected in the holistic macroeconomic view, delivers a better information basis for the recognition of opportunities and threats, which indicates a higher sensing performance. Based on this, it has to be assumed that:

> *Hypothesis H2d. The holistic macroeconomic view is positively associated with a company's sensing performance.*

4.2.1.3 Sensing Performance and Business Performance

Although Teece (2007) notes that some companies discover opportunities but still fail in their implementation and, consequently, in their performance, the majority of the studies point out that sensing in its various facets has an impact on the performance of the firm (e.g., Daft, Sormunen, & Parks, 1988; Tseng & Lee, 2014; Yang & Liu, 2012). According to these studies, successful companies generate a better understanding of their environment by sensing, and are therefore able to adapt better to market changes. By investigating the dynamic capabilities, Tseng and Lee (2014) found that there is a specific link between sensing and organizational performance. According to them, a company that exhibits a high sensing performance is more able to detect the dynamics in the market, which builds the fundament for any management decision, and therefore leads to an effective and efficient responsiveness concerning environmental changes. This, in turn, results in a good business performance (Tseng & Lee, 2014; Yang & Liu, 2012). Building on this, the hypothesis is:

Hypothesis H3. Sensing performance is positively associated with a company's business performance.

4.2.1.4 *Differences in Sensing concerning the Environmental Dynamism*

High levels of environmental dynamism are accompanied by a strong erosion of competitive advantages, and might therefore reduce the relevance of existing operational processes (Winter, 2003). For these reasons, dynamic capabilities might have more significance for organizations in high dynamic markets, where operational processes need to be adjusted more frequently (Barreto, 2010). Moreover, in low dynamic environments, dynamic capabilities might even lead to inappropriate changes (Teece, Pisano, & Shuen, 1997). Thus, it can be assumed that the higher the environmental dynamism, the stronger the effect of dynamic capabilities. Transfering this to the sensing concept of this study implies that the sensing activities in high dynamic environments have a higher impact on the sensing performance and consequently the business performance than they have in environments with low dynamism:

Hypothesis H4a. The higher the level of environmental dynamism, the stronger the impact of sensing activities on sensing performance.

Hypothesis H4b. The higher the level of environmental dynamism, the stronger the effect of sensing performance on business performance.

4.2.2 Derivation of the Hypotheses of Model 2 – Differences between Sensing Opportunities and Sensing Threats

As introduced in Chapter 1.4.2, almost no attention has been paid to the analysis of factors forming the interpretation of market information (Milliken, 1990; O'Reilly, 1982; Sutcliffe, 1997; Vandenbosch, Saatcioglu, & Fay, 2006), especially in regard to potential differences in sensing threats and sensing opportunities (Anderson & Nichols, 2007). This issue is addressed by looking at various environmental information sources and their different effects on the sensing of threats as opposed to the sensing of opportunities. As mentioned in Chapter 3.3.2, the classification of environmental information depends on the information richness, controllability, and information diversity (Anderson & Nichols, 2007; White, Varadarajan, & Dacin, 2003). Therefore, the question to ask is whether the environmental source, or the information from the environmental source, has such a characteristic, and therefore tends to have a different effect on whether it is sensed as being an opportunity or a threat. Thereby, the dependent construct "sensing performance" needed to be divided into "sensing opportunities" and "sensing threats", and hypotheses have been examined separately for each aspect of the sensing performance. In order to complete the picture all environmental sources have been set in relation to both dimensions of sensing performance. The gathering and analysis mode has not been addressed in Model 2, since there were no theoretical assumptions which would have led to profound hypotheses. For reasons of clarity, environmental dynamism has not been examined in this model.

Figure 4 provides an overview of the examined relationships of Model 2. The concrete derivation of this model's hypotheses will be described in the following sections. The derivation of the hypotheses is partially based on explanations by Anderson and Nichols (2007).

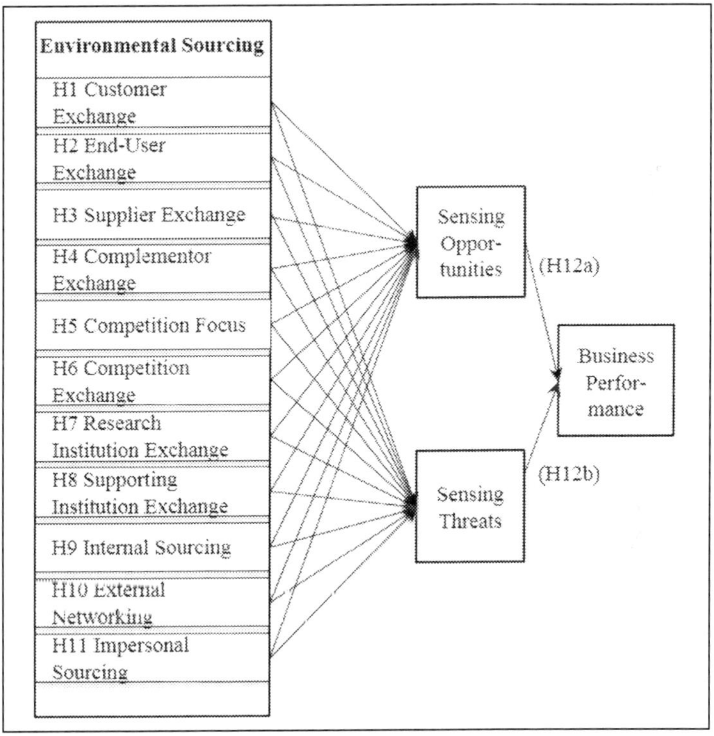

Figure 4 - Overall Model 2 - Environmental Sourcing Differences between Sensing Opportunities and Sensing Threats

While Figure 5 provides an overview of the hypothesized effects of the different environmental sourcings on sensing opportunities, and of sensing opportunities on business performance,

Figure 6 illustrates the effects of different environmental sourcings on sensing threats and of sensing threats on business performance.

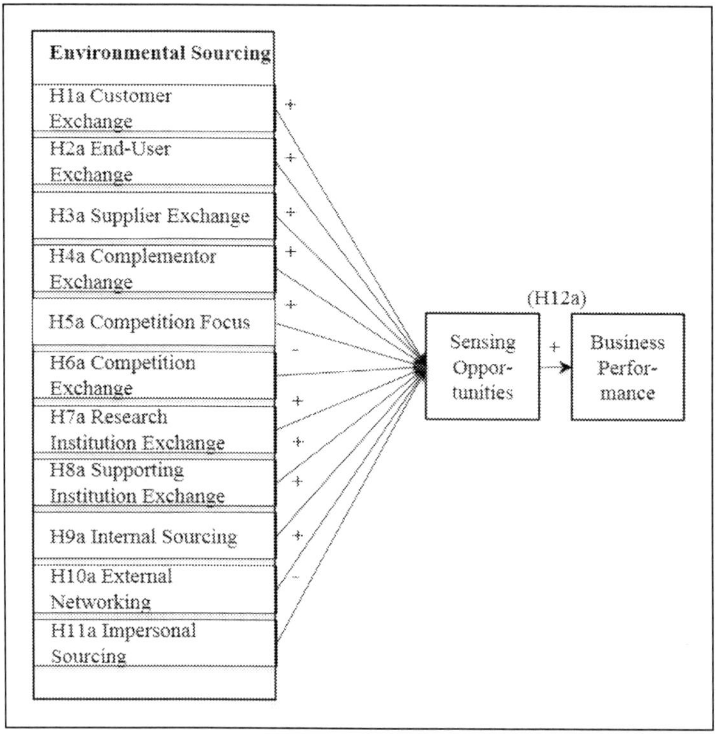

Figure 5 - Hypotheses regarding Sensing Opportunities

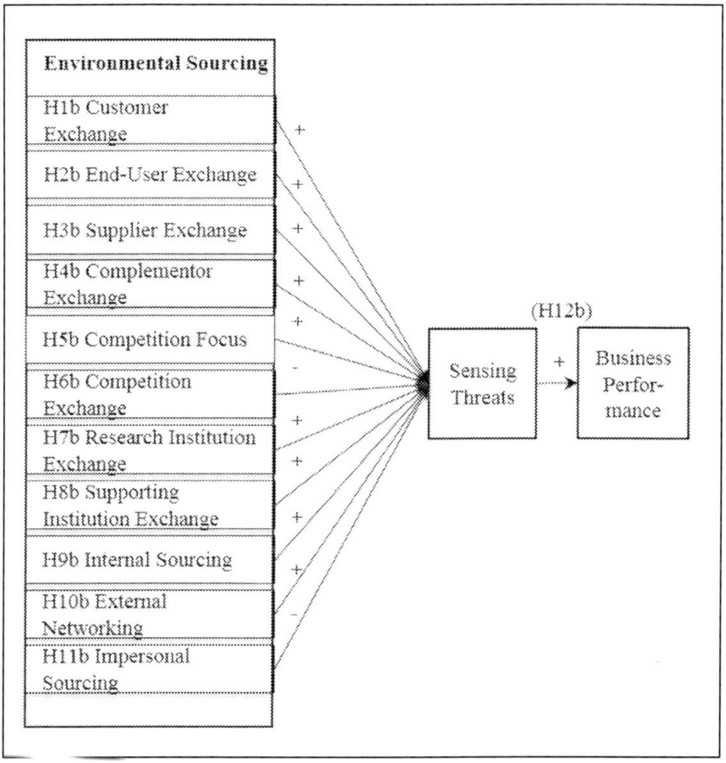

Figure 6 - Hypotheses regarding Sensing Threats

4.2.2.1 *Environmental Sourcing, Sensing Opportunities, and Sensing Threats*

In this section the hypotheses of different environmental sourcings will be derived separately for each part of the sensing performance.

Value Chain Partners and the Sensing of Opportunities and Threats

As mentioned in the hypotheses derivation section of Model 1, customer exchange, end-user exchange, and supplier exchange lead to a higher market orientation. Based on this generated knowledge and the improved understanding of such value chain partners, new business opportunities or business threats, such as new customer preferences, could be identified, indicating a better sensing capability, which means a better sensing of opportunities and threats (Harmancioglu, Grinstein, & Goldman, 2010; Hurmelinna-Laukkanen, 2012).

It cannot be learned from the literature whether there are differences between sensing threats and sensing opportunities in regard to supplier exchange and end-user exchange. Looking at the classification criteria for threats and opportunties as described in the theoretical foundation section (Chapter 3.3.2.), no specific manifestation in information richness, controllability, or information diversity can be found in these sources. Since the literature (Kohli, Jaworski, & Kumar, 1993; Matsuno, Mentzer, and Rentz, 2000) suggests that an exchange with end users or suppliers leads to a higher market orientation, and market orientation implies close contact with environmental changes, it is assumed that this will also lead to a higher sensing capability, meaning a better sensing of opportunities and threats.

The only source which might have a different and potentially even stronger effect in regard to sensing opportunities as opposed to sensing threats is customer exchange. Customers are among the most important information sources, especially in regard to the generation of new and innovative ideas (Harmancioglu, Grinstein, & Goldman, 2010; Hyland, Marceau, & Sloan, 2006; Robbinson &

Stubberud, 2011). Lukas and Ferrell (2000) found that a customer-oriented firm launched more "new-to-the-world" products, and thus had a greater amount of breakthrough innovations, which indicates the discovery of opportunities. The more frequently the partners interact, the more they can develop an understanding of each other's needs, and thus interpret the tacit knowledge (Cavusgil et al., 2003) residing inside the company's system (information about cultural values, for example) (Harmancioglu, Grinstein, & Goldman, 2010). With information like this, the company is able to gain insight into the latent needs and decision processes of customers, and can therefore discover new market opportunities (Harmancioglu, Grinstein, & Goldman, 2010). Since the customer segment is considered a reliable source (in comparison to the competitor sector, for example) (Auster & Choo, 1993), the perceived controllability is high, which also leads to a situation tending to be perceived more as an opportunity than a threat (White, Varadarajan, & Dacin, 2003).

Therefore the following is assumed:

Hypothesis H1a. Customer exchange is positively associated with a company's sensing of opportunities.

Hypothesis H1b. Customer exchange is positively associated with a company's sensing of threats.

Hypothesis H1c: Customer exchange is more positively associated with a company's sensing of opportunities than a company's sensing of threats.

Hypothesis H2a. End-user exchange is positively associated with a company's sensing of opportunities.

Hypothesis H2b. End-user exchange is positively associated with a company's sensing of threats.

Hypothesis H3a. Supplier exchange is positively associated with a company's sensing of opportunities.

Hypothesis H3b. Supplier exchange is positively associated with a company's sensing of threats.

Complementors and the Sensing of Opportunities and Threats

As mentioned in the hypotheses derivation part of Model 1, there has been considerably less attention paid to a further market participant relevant to exchange: the provider of complementary goods. As many companies experience dependency in this area, a complementary goods provider might be a good source of information on changes in the market. This information might help companies to identify new developments in their business environment more easily, indicating a better sensing capability, which means a better sensing of opportunities and threats (Teece, 2007).

In the literature, there is no indication to be found that there might be a different effect of complementor exchange on the sensing of threats or the sensing of opportunities. Since information quality, reliability, and scope from a complementors' exchange may vary in any direction, no clear differentiating effect can be assigned to this exchange channel (White, Varadarajan, & Dacin, 2003). That is why it can be assumed that complementor exchange affects both the sensing of threats and the sensing of opportunities to the same extent. Hence:

Hypothesis H4a. Complementor exchange is positively associated with a company's sensing of opportunities.

Hypothesis H4b. Complementor exchange is positively associated with a company's sensing of threats.

Competitors and the Sensing of Opportunities and Threats

As early as 1980, Porter pointed out the importance of considering the competition to be able to anticipate competitors' actions. Since researchers (Kohli & Jaworski,

1990; Matsuno, Mentzer, & Rentz, 2000) confirm that there is a higher market orientation when competition is observed regularly, it is to be assumed that this competitor orientation or focus also leads to a better sensing of opportunities and threats. This relation has already been addressed in Model 1, and will be examined in a more differentiated way here in Model 2. Since no explanation or research study could be found concerning differences of competition focus between the sensing of threats and the sensing of opportunities, it might be that there are no differences. This leads to the assumption that competition focus affects both the sensing of threats and the sensing of opportunities to the same extent.

On the basis of a literature review on this topic, it is considered to be appropriate to include the effect of competition exchange in this model. In the literature, there are contradictory views as to whether the relationship between competition exchange and the sensing of opportunities and threats is positive or negative, because cooperation with competitors brings with it a certain potential for conflict. On the one hand, contact with competitors could enhance know-how in the organization, and may therefore help identify threats or opportunities (Hurmelinna-Laukkanen, 2012; Jung-Erceg et al., 2007), but on the other hand, information on market developments, such as new customer segments or new regulations emerging, might lead to a competitive advantage, and may result in competitors being reluctant to pass on this information. In turn, this might lead to protective behavior between competitors, which would cast doubt on the value of the information exchanged (Hurmelinna-Laukkanen, 2012). Since companies do not, for their part, wish to disclose sensitive information that is related to success, but would like to get that information from their competitors, it can be assumed that companies taking part in a strong competitive exchange might fail to recognize relevant market developments, and that their sensing capability might therefore be diminished by a reduced sensing of opportunities and threats.

One has to wonder whether this effect might be different depending on whether it is a question of a threat or an opportunity. The "competition" as a source is linked with a particularly large perceived uncertainty (Daft et al., 1988). In general, it is difficult to obtain reliable information from or about competitors (Auster & Choo,

1993; Montgomery, Moore, & Urbany, 2005). This deficit would lead to the management seeing a strategic issue as less controllable, and hence tending to categorize upcoming issues from competitive exchange as threats rather than opportunities (Jackson & Dutton, 1988). The availability of information could reduce this effect (White, Varadarajan, & Dacin, 2003), but firms would not be able to gather enough information from the competition. Consequently, the perceived controllability would decrease, and the probability of the management categorizing an ambiguous issue as a threat would increase. This conclusion is supported by what is known as the "threat bias", where managers tend to see issues as a threat unless there is strong evidence for seeing them as an opportunity (Jackson & Dutton, 1988).

By combining the general decreasing effect of competition exchange on the sensing of opportunities and threats with the fact that information from the competitor is considered more of a threat than an opportunity, it can be concluded that there might be a less negative influence on the sensing of threats than on the sensing of opportunities. As far as it is known, this has never been empirically proven before, and will be shown by the results of this study.

In line with the above arguments, the following hypotheses can be suggested:

> *Hypothesis H5a. Competition focus is positively associated with a company's sensing of opportunities.*

> *Hypothesis H5b. Competition focus is positively associated with a company's sensing of threats.*

> *Hypothesis H6a. Competition exchange is negatively associated with a company's sensing of opportunities.*

> *Hypothesis H6b. Competition exchange is negatively associated with a company's sensing of threats.*

Hypothesis H6c. Competition exchange is more negatively associated with a company's sensing of opportunities than a company's sensing of threats.

Institutions and the Sensing of Opportunities and Threats

The large majority of institutional cooperations are formed with universities. These cooperative relationships are a source of knowledge for both small and large companies and firms and universities make more of an effort to take an active part in such relationships because they have no need to feel defensive about losing potentially important information due to a competitive advantage (Fey & Birkinshaw, 2005; Möller & Rajala, 2007), as already mentioned concerning Model 1. Ellonen, Wikström, and Jantunen (2009) note in their study that companies that work together closely with universities have a good sensing capability, which means that these companies are successful in sensing opportunities and threats. Since the exchange with research institutions is mainly geared toward generating new ideas or interesting business opportunities, the sensing effect might be mainly derived from the sensing of opportunities, which implicates a higher positive effect of research institution exchange on the sensing of opportunities than on the sensing of threats.

Concerning Model 1, it was further suggested that supporting institutional structures have a major impact on the market as they may support innovation and thus influence the competition. Since the assets and knowledge of supporting institutions could be integrated into new value-added combinations, thereby shaping the market (Teece, 2007), these institutions might play a relevant role in market analysis and, because of their purpose, the exchange with these institutions might primarily help with the discovery of opportunities, which would probably mean a higher positive effect on the sensing of opportunities than on the sensing of threats. Based on these arguments, the following can be assumed:

Hypothesis H7a. Research institution exchange is positively associated with a company's sensing of opportunities.

Hypothesis H7b. Research institution exchange is positively associated with a company's sensing of threats.

Hypothesis H7c. Research institution exchange is more positively associated with a company's sensing of opportunities than a company's sensing of threats.

Hypothesis H8a. Supporting institution exchange is positively associated with a company's sensing of opportunities.

Hypothesis H8b. Supporting institution exchange is positively associated with a company's sensing of threats.

Hypothesis H8c. Supporting institution exchange is more positively associated with a company's sensing of opportunities than a company's sensing of threats.

Internal Sourcing and the Sensing of Opportunities and Threats

Regarding the internal sourcing hypotheses of Model 1, it has been explained in depth that people can be valuable information sources in the business environment, particularly those who are in direct contact with external constituents within the company. Furthermore, the great importance which Matsuno, Mentzer, and Rentz (2000) attached to internal sources for keeping track of external developments might imply that this sourcing also drives a company's sensing capability, and therefore the sensing of opportunities and threats. According to the richness and diversity of the information from this information source, it can be assumed that companies are more likely to sense opportunities than threats by using this environmental sourcing channel (White, Varadarajan, & Dacin, 2003). Hence:

Hypothesis H9a. Internal sourcing is positively associated with a company's sensing of opportunities.

Hypothesis H9b. Internal sourcing is positively associated with a company's sensing of threats.

Hypothesis H9c. Internal sourcing is more positively associated with a company's sensing of opportunities than with a company's sensing of threats.

External Networking and the Sensing of Opportunities and Threats

Hitt et al. (2001), and Helm and Gritsch (2014) suggest that external network contacts could be particularly rich sources of information on the environment. Following their argumentation, networks create continuity in social contacts and dialog, and can supply the latest information on market developments, and thus increase an organization's sensing capability and therefore the sensing of opportunities and threats.

In their study on the behavior of "champions"[3], Howell and Shea (2001) found that the personal network can be seen as the most effective source when scanning for new ideas. The results of the research by Cavusgil et al. (2003) suggest that due to the intensive use of the network and the associated tacit knowledge, opportunities are identified more quickly and efficiently, which in turn can lead to more innovations (Cavusgil et al., 2003). These findings provide the first indication that networks are suitable for sensing opportunities. Another argument in favor of the preferred sensing of opportunities is the diversity of information in a network, which

3 Champions are defined as "individuals, who informally emerge in an organization and make a decisive contribution to the innovation by actively and enthusiastically promoting its progress through the critical stages" (Howell et al., 2005: 642).

goes hand in hand with an increasing sensing of opportunities (Anderson & Nichols, 2007). Although Anderson (2008) found no correlation between the strength of connections and the diversity of information, he was able to demonstrate that managers with a larger social network can gather a greater diversity of data. This could be explained by the fact that an actor can easily switch to another personal source (Anderson, 2008; Cross & Sproull, 2004). In summary, it can be said that companies that maintain intensive connections in the network might have a stronger effect on the sensing of opportunities than on the sensing of threats.

In line with the above reasons, the following might be assumed:

> *Hypothesis H10a. External networking is positively associated with a company's sensing of opportunities.*
>
> *Hypothesis H10b. External networking is positively associated with a company's sensing of threats.*
>
> *Hypothesis H10c. External networking is more positively associated with a company's sensing of opportunities than with a company's sensing of threats.*

Impersonal Sourcing and the Sensing of Opportunities and Threats

Many companies seem to use the obvious external information source of impersonal sourcing. On the basis of the hypothesis derivation concerning impersonal sourcing of Model 1, one could deduce that media sourcing delivers less valuable information as regards recognizing opportunities or threats in the business environment, and might therefore not provide much support for a company's sensing capability. Since impersonal sources only provide limited feedback and low information richness (Auster & Choo, 1994; Daft & Lengel, 1986), and according to the "threat bias" theory (Jackson & Dutton, 1988), whereby managers perceive ambiguous issues as more of a threat unless there is strong evidence for them to do otherwise, members of the organization might interpret an issue from this source as more of a threat than an opportunity. Therefore, the increased use of impersonal sources, and the low diversity of the data gathered could contribute more to the detection of threats and less to the identification of opportunities.

In line with the above reasons, the following might be assumed:

> *Hypothesis H11a. Impersonal sourcing is negatively associated with a company's sensing of opportunities.*
>
> *Hypothesis H11b. Impersonal sourcing is negatively associated with a company's sensing of threats.*
>
> *Hypothesis H11c. Impersonal sourcing is less negatively associated with a company's sensing of threats than a company's sensing of opportunities.*

4.2.2.2 Sensing Opportunities, Sensing Threats, and Business Performance

According to the findings of Teece (2007) or Tseng and Lee (2014), which have been fully explained for Model 1, there seems to be a specific link between sensing and a company's business performance. After having illustrated the effect of sensing on the business performance in Model 1, a further question arises as to whether sensing threats and sensing opportunities might each have a different impact on business performance.

Dutton (1992) deals extensively with the issue of opportunity recognition or construction and their effects on organizational change. She shows that the assessment of a situation or condition as an opportunity has a psychological impact on managers and members of an organization. She postulates, for example, that individuals who see an issue as an opportunity receive more support to exploit it, because other people are inspired by positive emotions and values as well (Dutton, 1992).

In her study, this indicates that employees in the organization are ready to perform and contribute to an improvement in performance when an opportunity is detected. Further, she argues that an "opportunity" label leads to a more future-oriented attitude, and even if the company was less successful in the past, a positive new beginning could be signaled which is collectively motivating. The future orientation also gives the individuals a greater degree of freedom in thought and action, which leads to the enhancement of individuals' willingness to invest resources (Dutton, 1992). If one also takes a look at the results of Ngo and O'Cass (2012), who postulate a positive relation between marketing resources and the company's performance, it can be seen that greater commitments of corporate resources lead to better business performance. These aspects might also suggest that the discovery or interpretation of opportunities within the company promotes the motivation of the members of the organization and their willingness to support strategic issues. In turn, this could lead to better business performance.

Concerning the response to a threat, there is a divergent perspective that has been widely discussed in the literature (Anderson & Nichols, 2007; Chattopadhyay et al., 2001; White, Varadarajan, & Dacin, 2003). First, the prospect theory assumes that losses are weighted more than gains, and that individuals are willing to take more risks when they are confronted with possible disadvantages (Kahneman & Tversky, 1979). Therefore, the responses to risks are more extreme than the responses to gains (Tversky & Kahneman, 1986). This would lead to a manager committing more resources when confronted with an issue related to a threat, for example (White, Varadarajan, & Dacin, 2003). Consequently, the willingness to make a risky response could also result in greater commitments of company resources, and thus lead to better business performance.

However, the threat-rigidity thesis assumes that problems lead to stress and anxiety for individuals, and that they are also aware of the probability of loss. As a result, the actions of an organization are less flexible and less diverse, because the controllability is limited under these circumstances, and the power is more concentrated or lies at higher levels in the company. Here, the decision-makers often rely on very familiar responses and more rigid structures to improve the controllability. Since flexibility is very important in response to environmental changes, this rigid behavior can be a disadvantage for the performance of the organization. As a consequence, the performance of the firm could decline because of the increased sensing of threats (Staw, Sandelands, & Dutton, 1981).

This diverse argumentation based on the two theoretical strings "prospect theory" (Kahneman & Tversky, 1979) and the "threat-rigidity" theory (Staw, Sandelands, & Dutton, 1981) shows the multidimensionality of threats and opportunities best (Jackson & Dutton, 1988; Thomas, Clark, & Gioia, 1993). Although very few researchers have integrated these two theories into their multidimensional conceptual models examining the effects of threats and opportunities on organizational actions (Ocasio, 1995), no empirical test of such a model has been reported, except by Chattopadhyay et al., 2001. Though both views have their justification, there is a research stream (House, Rousseau, & Thomas-Hunt, 1995; Katsuhiko, 2007; Ruefli et al., 1999; Thaler & Johnson, 1990) which argues that prospect theory was inferred from laboratory experiments with individuals, and did not investigate the risk behavior on an organizational level. Following these arguments, the threat-rigidity theory seems to fit the context of this study better. Building on this, the hypotheses are as follows:

Hypothesis H12a. Sensing opportunities is positively associated with a company's business performance.

Hypothesis H12b. Sensing threats is positively associated with a company's business performance.

Hypothesis H12c. Sensing of opportunities is more positively associated with a company's business performance than with a company's business performance in regard to sensing threats.

5 Methodical Foundations and Operationalization

5.1 Methodical Foundations

5.1.1 Basics of Structural Equation Modeling

The structural equation analysis, which is used for this study, is one of the multivariate analysis methods examining structure (Backhaus & Weiber, 2007). When there is a complex relation structure between manifest or latent variables, and the aim is to examine the effect correlations quantitatively, a structural equation analysis is recommended (Weiber & Mühlhaus, 2010). According to the fact that Model 1 includes a context variable ("environmental dynamism"), and both models in this study have a high complexity, the structural equation modeling seems to be ideal for quantitatively examining the cause-effect relationships. In contrast to classical regression analysis, with which unilateral correlations are estimated, structural equation analysis examines complex variable relations, which represent causal guesses about the relation structure between the variables considered. The variables in the hypotheses can therefore be independent but also dependent variables, like the "sensing performance" variable in Model 1 (Backhaus et al., 2011; Weiber & Mühlhaus, 2010). The structural model represents the relation between exogenous and endogenous constructs, while the measurement model describes the causal relationships between a construct and its indicators (Backhaus, Erichson, & Weiber, 2013).

5.1.2 Formative vs. Reflective Measurement

According to Blalock (1964), two kinds of measurement models can be used for the operationalization of constructs: either a reflective, or a formative measurement model.

Formative measurement models follow a regression analytical approach, with the special feature, however, that no empirical measurement values are available for the latent variables as dependent variables. Therefore, these variables have to be estimated in relation to other latent variables. In contrast to this, reflective measurement models follow a factor analytical approach, and assume that there are high correlations between measurement variables which are caused by the latent variable (Weiber & Mühlhaus, 2010).

Table 2 shows the concrete differences between reflective and formative measurement models. This table is based on Jarvis, MacKenzie, and Podsakof (2003), and Weiber and Mühlhaus (2010), and provides four essential criteria and their related implications, which serve as a decision base for identifying the right measurement model. These criteria are: the direction of causality between the construct and the respective indicators, the exchangeability of the indicators, the covariance between the indicators, and the integration of the indicators in a joint nomological network.

Criteria	Formative Measurement Model	Reflective Measurement Model
Direction of Causality	From the indicators to the the construct: – Indicators are defining characteristics of the construct – Characteristics of the indicators should lead to changes in the construct	From the construct to the indicators: – Indicators represent the facets of the construct – Changes in the construct should lead to changes in indicators' characteristics
Exchangeability of the Indicators	Indicators do not need to be exchangeable: – Indicators do not need to have the same content – The exclusion of an indicator could change the conceptual frame of the construct	Indicators should be exchangeable: – Indicators should share the same content or a joint topic – The exclusion of an indicator should not change the conceptual frame of the construct
Covariance between the Indicators	Indicators do not need to be co-varied	Indicators should be co-varied
Nomological Network of the Indicators	The nomological network of the indicators can be different – Indicators do not need to have the same antecedents and consequences	The nomological network of the indicators should not be different – Indicators need to have the same antecedents and consequences

Table 2 - Decision Criteria for the Identification of Formative and Reflective Measurement Variables

In the following, some explanations of the different characteristics of each measurement model as illustrated in the table above are provided.

As the name suggests, formative indicators form the construct, and are therefore not exchangeable. If an indicator is excluded, the conceptual frame of the construct changes. Therefore, each indicator is necessary to capture the full picture of the construct in this case. As a consequence, the indicators do not necessarily need to be co-varied, and do not need to have the same antecedents and consequences.

In contrast to formative indicators, reflective indicators reflect the characteristics of the construct, whereby a change in the construct's value simultaneously leads to a change in the indicator's value. Reflective indicators are more exchangeable because they are correlated, and their content is identical. In addition, the variation of an indicator leads to the variation of another indicator, meaning covariance. Therefore, the exclusion of an indicator has no effect on the conceptual framework or content of the construct. Further, reflective measured constructs have a joint nomological network, which means that the antecedents and consequences of the indicators are the same (Diamantopoulos & Winklhofer, 2001; MacKenzie, Podsakoff, & Podsakoff, 2011).

Although there is a prominent use of reflective measurement in the research, formative measurement models might have been correct in many cases (Fassott & Eggert, 2005; Weiber & Mühlhaus, 2010). In their meta-analysis of 25 articles, for instance, Fassott and Eggert (2005) discovered that most of the constructs have been handled as reflective, while the indicators have been formulated as if they were formative. By analyzing 34 articles from the *Journal of Marketing*, Eberl (2004) found that 11% of the constructs had been measured incorrectly as reflective instead of formative. Nevertheless, there are basic differences between these methods which should be considered in the analysis of a causal structure (Weiber & Mühlhaus, 2010), since a false specification can lead to a false statistical evaluation, not to mention incorrect research results, or implications for management

(Eberl, 2004; Weiber & Mühlhaus, 2010). Chapter 5.2, which covers the operationalization and measurement of the models used, will show why a reflective measurement model is used for this study.

5.1.3 Covariance-Based vs. Variance-Based Approaches

The different causality direction between the measurement variables and a latent variable makes it necessary to use different analysis instruments to examine the respective measurement model (formative or reflective). As observed above, reflective measurement models are verified with the confirmatory factor analysis, and formative measurement models are verified with a regression analytical approach. However, it must also be considered whether a covariance-based or variance-based approach should be used for the modeling and examination of a causal model (Weiber & Mühlhaus, 2010). Covariance analytical and variance analytical methods are often considered to be substitutive regarding the empirical analysis of causal models, but there are some basic differences.

The covariance-based method uses an integrated and simultaneous estimation of the causal structure of a model in total. What matters in this respect is not the reproduction of the original data (case values), but the reproduction of a variance-covariance matrix, which reflects the empirical measured relations between all measurement variables. Therefore, the covariance-based approach is one that tests the full set of variable relations, and is hence ideal for theory evaluation (Weiber & Mühlhaus, 2010).

In the case of missing information or a relatively small information base concerning the "true" causal structure, covariance-based analysis with statistical programs like LISREL or AMOS no longer works. Therefore, Wold (1966, 1980, 1982) initiated a different variance-analytical approach based on the reproduction of the original data matrix to obtain usable results from this "reduced" information base, called Partial Least Square (PLS). As the name suggests, this approach is based on a least square estimation, and can also be used for a small sample. Meanwhile, there are different statistical programs, such as LVPLS or SmartPLS, which use this approach (Weiber & Mühlhaus, 2010). While covariance-based approaches estimate the relations in the structural model based on the factor variance alone, and disregard the individual residual variance, the variance-based approach, like PLS, is additionally determined by the measurement error variance, and hence can only capture the relations in the structural model in a restricted way, in contrast to the covariance-based analysis, which provides very reliable estimates.

Since this empirical study has a large sample size, meaning that an extensive information base is given, and since the structural relationships should be reproduced as realistically as possible in order to provide a substantiated examination of theory-based hypotheses, the decision was made to select the "hard-modeling" covariance-based approach. Even if both covariance-based and variance-based approaches can model and examine both reflective and formative measurement models, covariance-based approaches are primarily intended to be used for reflective measurement models (Weiber & Mühlhaus, 2010).

5.2 Measures and Operationalization

As far as possible, existing measures were used to develop the items and scales. As only a few empirical studies have been carried out directly in regard to the sensing topic as part of the dynamic capabilities framework, existing items from related research contexts have been integrated, and adapted to fit the concept of this study. All of the relationships in Model 1 and 2 were measured according to the respondents' subjective assessment based on a six-point Likert scale. Referring to Fuchs and Diamantopoulos (2009), a single-item measurement for most constructs was used, since most constructs are specific and unidimensional in terms of Rossiter (2002).

Table 3 provides an overview of all items used, followed by the description of the respective measures.

Environmental Sourcing

Customer Exchange

1. How often, compared to your competitors, does your company meet direct customers to figure out what products or services could be of value to them in the future?

End-User Exchange

2. How often, compared to your competitors, does your company meet end users to figure out what products or services could be of value to them in the future?

Supplier Exchange

3. In our company, we exchange with suppliers very often about market developments and their plans and activities.

Complementor Exchange

4. In our company, we exchange with providers of complementary goods very often about market developments and their plans and activities.

Competition Focus

5. We constantly benchmark ourselves against our competitors.
6. We have extensive information about our competition.

Competition Exchange

7. In our company, we exchange with competitors very often about market developments and their plans and activities.

External Networking

8. To what extent do employees of your company actively participate in business networks?
9. How strongly is your company engaged in associations?

Impersonal Sourcing

10. To what extent does your company use media to be able to estimate market developments better?

Research Institution Exchange

11. In our company, we very often exchange information with universities or other research institutions about market developments and their plans and activities.

Supporting Institution Exchange

12. In our company, we very often exchange information with supporting institutions about market developments and their plans and activities.

Internal Sourcing

13. We operate very intensively in internal market research.

Environmental Gathering & Analysis Mode

Gathering and Analysis Intensity

14. We take a lot of time for gathering and analyzing market information.
15. If something is not clear, we analyze it again.
16. Before we make a decision in our company due to market changes, we need to conduct extensive research and analysis.

Systematic Approach

17. To what extent does your company undertake a concentrated search for changes in the market environment?
18. In our company, market information is gathered and analyzed according to a clear structured approach.
19. The gathering and analysis of market information happens continuously.
20. In our company, new relevant information always leads to a reconsideration of our own decisions.

Pragmatic Approach

21. I would describe our analysis methods as being very pragmatic.

Holistic Macroeconomic View

22. In our company, we have regular meetings to discuss general macroeconomic information (e.g., interest rates, exchange rates, GDP, industry growth rates, inflation rates) and their effect on our company.
23. In our company, we have regular meetings to discuss the regulatory framework and its effect on our company.
24. In our company, we have regular meetings to discuss political developments (e.g., intergovernmental initiatives, governmental fiscal planning) and their effect on our company.
25. In our company, we have regular meetings to discuss general social trends (e.g., environmental awareness, emerging lifestyles) and their effect on our company.
26. In our company, we have regular meetings to discuss demographical trends (e.g., ageing society) and their effect on our company.

Endogenous Variables

Sensing Performance

27. As soon as an opportunity for our company arose from market changes, we were always the first to recognize this opportunity in the last three years.
28. As soon as a threat to our company arose from market changes, we were always the first to recognize this threat in the last three years.
29. In comparison to our competition, we recognized far fewer opportunities in the last three years. (reverse-coded)

Business Performance	
30. How would you evaluate the development of your company in comparison to your main competitors in terms of sales revenue growth?	
31. How would you evaluate the development of your company in comparison to your main competitors in terms of market share?	
32. How would you evaluate the development of your company in comparison to your main competitors in terms of profitability?	
Moderating Variable	
Environmental Dynamism	
33. Our company needs to change its products or services frequently to be able to keep pace with the competition.	
34. Products or services quickly become obsolete in our market.	
35. Technology changes faster in our market than in other markets.	
36. Customer needs differ strongly between the different customer segments in our market.	
Control Variables	
Firm Size	
37. What is the number of persons currently employed at your company?	
Risk-taking	
38. In our company, we have a disproportionate tendency to take risks.	

Table 3 - Variables

Sensing Activities Measures

To examine a company's sensing capability, the activities affecting the ability to sense opportunities and threats have to be measured. As mentioned in the introduction sections (Chapter 1.4 and Chapter 3.3), the sensing capability has been divided into the sensing activities, which consists of the "environmental sourcing" and the "environmental gathering and analysis mode", and the actual sensing performance of a company. To capture the sourcing activities, items from the MO and MARKOR scale have been used (Kohli, Jaworski, & Kumar, 1993; Matsuno, Mentzer, & Rentz, 2000). For the "environmental gathering and analysis mode", items have been derived from Aguilar's (1967) and Daft and Weick's (1984) concepts of environmental scanning. These items have been reformulated and adapted to fit the understanding of and perspective on sensing prevalent in the literature (Barreto, 2010; Teece, 2007, 2012). Furthermore, other relevant items have been included regarding the concept of sensing which were derived from suggestions found in the research on dynamic capabilities (Ambrosini & Bowman, 2009; Barreto, 2010; Teece, 2007, 2012).

Environmental Sourcing Measures

In this study, the 'environmental sourcing' dimension was measured with thirteen items. The first questions were derived from the MARKOR and MO scale, and relate to the exchange with the typical market players (customer, supplier, end-user, and competitor) (referring to questions 1, 2, 3, 5, 6, 7 in the table). The aspects of external network exchange, internal sourcing, and impersonal sourcing were derived from Matsuno, Mentzer, and Rentz 's (2000) framework (questions 8, 9, 10, 13). The literature on dynamic capabilities and, above all, Teece (2007) also suggest focusing on complementors and institutions as environmental information sources in order to gain a sustainable competitive advantage over time, which has also been integrated in Model 1 and 2 (questions 4, 11, 12).

Environmental Gathering and Analysis Mode Measures

Since the aim of this thesis is to figure out activities as specifically as possible, it was also necessary to break the environmental gathering and analysis mode down according to literature recommendations (Aguilar, 1967; Kirzner, 1973; Teece, 2007; Matsuno, Mentzer, & Rentz, 2000; Flores et al., 2012) to the "gathering and analysis intensity", the "systematic approach", the "pragmatic approach", and the "holistic macroeconomic view" (questions 14 - 26). While the measures for the gathering and analysis intensity have been derived from Kirzner (1973), and Teece (2007), the measures for the systematic approach are based on Aguilar (1967), and Flores et al. (2012). The measure for the pragmatic approach is based on the outcome of the pre-study (10 top management interviews) and pre-test (consultation of top managers and academic experts) of this study, confirming that everybody understands the same thing by a pragmatic approach, as defined in the hypotheses derivation section in Chapter 4.2.1. The inclusion and operationalization of the holistic macroeconomic view comes from Matsuno, Mentzer, and Rentz (2000).

Sensing Performance Measures

Based on the understanding of sensing presented here, which has been derived from Teece's (2007) and Schreyögg & Kliesch-Eberl's (2007) concept of sensing as mentioned in Chapter 3.2, useful operationalization efforts were found in the market-orientation scale by Kohli, Jaworski, and Kumar (1993), and Matsuno, Mentzer, and Rentz (2000). Then the sensing performance of Model 1 was measured as the actual achievement of sensing opportunities and threats (questions 27 – 29), to visualize the effect of a company's sensing capability.

For Model 2, this sensing performance was divided into the two dimensions sensing opportunities (question 27) and sensing threats (question 28).

Business Performance Measures

In line with Anand and Ward (2004), and Richard et al. (2009), market share, sales growth, and profit as the organization's outcomes were used for business performance (questions 30 – 32). The performance development was investigated over the last three years, as this represents the success of a company better than current year figures. It also means that large and small companies can be compared more easily. Each aspect of the company's business performance was measured as a single item with the belief that the respondents had answered truthfully concerning the business situation of their companies, as the absolute confidentiality of this survey was guaranteed.

Environmental Dynamism Measures

The environmental dynamism construct is measured based on items from Talke and O'Connor (2011), and Baum and Wally (2003), who expanded Kohli and Jaworski's (1990) market dynamism scale with the technology dynamism in order to give a more comprehensive picture of the business environment (questions 33 – 36).

Control Variables

Company size and risk-taking have been included as controls to ensure that the relationships examined were not guided by distortion effects (questions 37, 38). As a control variable, company size might particularly have an influence on the sensing of opportunities and threats, as larger organizations may tend to be more successful at sensing threats or opportunities because of their greater slack resources, and the fact that they have more specialists, such as risk management officers. Company size was controlled further in terms of business performance, as it has been suggested by many researchers that size can have an impact on organizational practices because it often stands for organizational complexity (e.g. Smith, Collins, & Clark, 2005).

The control variable risk-taking was included in the models, since this might have an impact on sensing relations, as companies which are more willing to take risks might also be able to sense opportunities and threats more easily (Jambulingam, Kathuria, & Doucette, 2005).

6 A New Empirical Study

6.1 Research Design of the Study

6.1.1 Survey Development and Questionnaire Concept

The questionnaire was generated based on the procedures recommended by Churchill (1979), and Gerbing and Anderson (1988). The method of investigation applied in this study evolved through a combination of exploratory qualitative interviews, a review of the literature on sensing, and a survey pretest.

The qualitative interviews were conducted with corporate executives from different German companies of different sizes and from different sectors. These companies with contrasting characteristics were selected so that potential differences concerning the aspects investigated could be identified. This method is also supported by Eisenhardt (1989). The main aim of the interviews was to match the practical viewpoint with the literature-based model, and also to gain perspectives from different firms and sectors. Thus, the hypotheses of both models could be logically evaluated and operationalization could be pre-screened (Atteslander, 1984). The interviews were conducted according to typical case study approaches (Yin, 2014), a method supported by many researchers (e.g. Eisenhardt, 1989), in order to explore and examine the theory.

The aim here was not to create case studies, but just to use this method as a professional analysis tool to verify the theory. The results that emerged helped to make the main survey more practical and focused. By employing this approach, literature-based concepts, constructs, or items which have been examined under different conditions from those of this study (other regions or countries, or specific industries, for example) could be correctly transferred to the context here.

To create the standardized questionnaire, care was taken to use a potential common-method bias, meaning systematical distortions of the response behavior.

According to Podsakoff et al. (2003), the following aspects of the questionnaire were integrated to prevent the common-method bias:

- Guarantee of anonymity for the respondents at the beginning of the survey
- An appealing and varied survey layout
- Different scale descriptions
- No item-ambiguity
- Separation of the questions on dependent and independent variables in the questionnaire

The adapted, structured questionnaire was subsequently pretested by various academic research experts and top managers who were representative for the sample. It was therefore possible to obtain information on the simplicity, neutrality and clarity of the questionnaire (Helm & Glück, 1997). According to the experts' remarks, there was no doubt about any unambiguous understanding of the questions. The experts' remarks were aligned with the theory and past research outcomes, and it was thus possible to draw up a suitable and unequivocal questionnaire.

To conduct this survey, the top executives were invited personally by email to respond to the questions online. An online survey was chosen because it is an appropriate method of selecting standardized, quantitative data (Kerlinger, 1979; Henning-Thurau & Dallwitz-Wegner, 2002). In contrast to other research approaches, a mail or online survey has the advantage of a wide reach, no interviewer bias, low distribution bias, as well as cost and time savings (Sittimalakorn & Hart, 2004). To provide the respondents with an incentive to participate, they were promised a summary of the results by mail.

6.1.2 Sample Selection and Description

To conduct this study, members of the executive board and top management of German companies were contacted. They were required to have the ability to assess sensing activities, environmental dynamism, the company's actual sensing of opportunities and threats, and their company's business performance. Even if top management do not perform all the examined activities directly, their position means that they are still involved and well informed about such activities, since related changes have an impact on company performance. Consequently, the data is generated by an informed single source. The persons contacted represented the respective company (Day & Lord, 1988). Research assumes that persons from the top management serve as key informants on this topic, so the methods used in previous studies, where the top managers of companies served as the main informants (e.g., Danneels, 2008), were applied.

The sample frame used was the DAFNE company database. In a first step, the sample was narrowed down based on the company size (> 100 employees). The organizational structures of smaller companies are less formal, which makes it quite difficult for the respondents to provide a clear and valid assessment of sensing practices used throughout the organization (Foss, Lyngsie, & Zahra, 2013). Of the recieved questionnaires, some needed to be excluded because of missing values or "speedster" response behavior[4]. When the return rate to the original sample was compared, no relevant non-response bias or incentive effect was found.

[4] In this context a speedster is a respondent who clicks through the questionnaire quite rapidly and chooses the same answer category for each question, regardless of what might be the right answer.

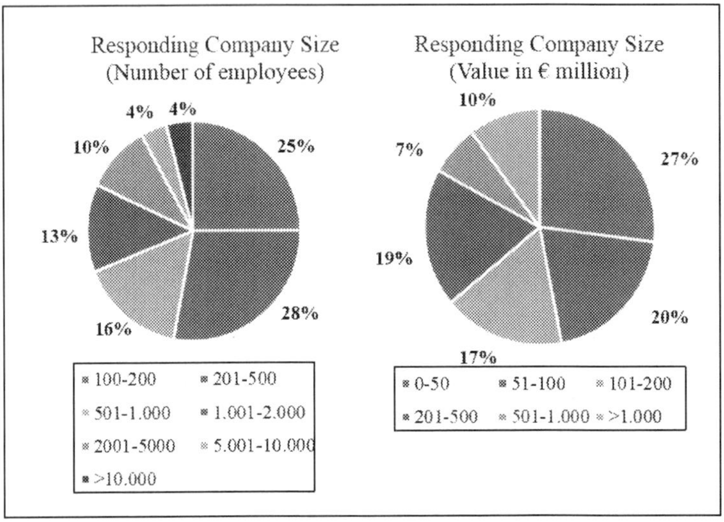

Figure 7, Responding Companies

Figure 7 illustrates the responding companies classified by company size. This figure shows that all company sizes are well represented by the set of respondents, which is similar to the original sample distribution.

6.2 Empirical Evaluation of the Structural Equation Models

6.2.1 Model 1 – The Sensing Capability

6.2.1.1 Data Analysis

The hypotheses of Model 1 were examined by employing a structural equation modeling with maximum likelihood estimation. To use a maximum likelihood estimation in the context of a covariance-based structural analysis, it is first necessary to assess if a multi-normal distribution of the data is given (Weiber & Mühlhaus, 2010). According to the Kolmogorov-Smirnoff test, which indicates a normal distribution on an indicator level, and the test of the multivariate kurtosis coefficient (Browne, 1982) for the multivariate normal distribution, it can be confirmed that there is no serious infringement of the normal distribution of the data (Bollen, 1989; Weiber & Mühlhaus, 2010).

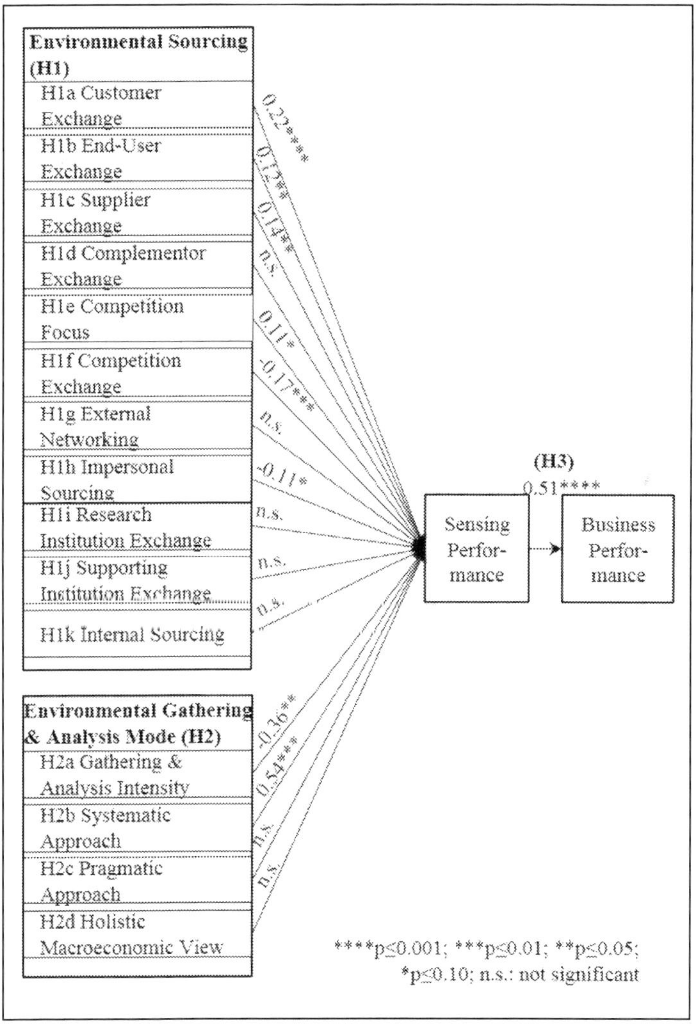

Figure 7 - Structural Equation Modeling Results for the Overall Sample (Model 1a)

First, Hypothesis group 1 (environmental sourcing), Hypothesis group 2 (environmental gathering & analysis mode), Hypothesis 3 and their subhypotheses were analyzed using the structural equation modeling (Model 1a – Figure 8).

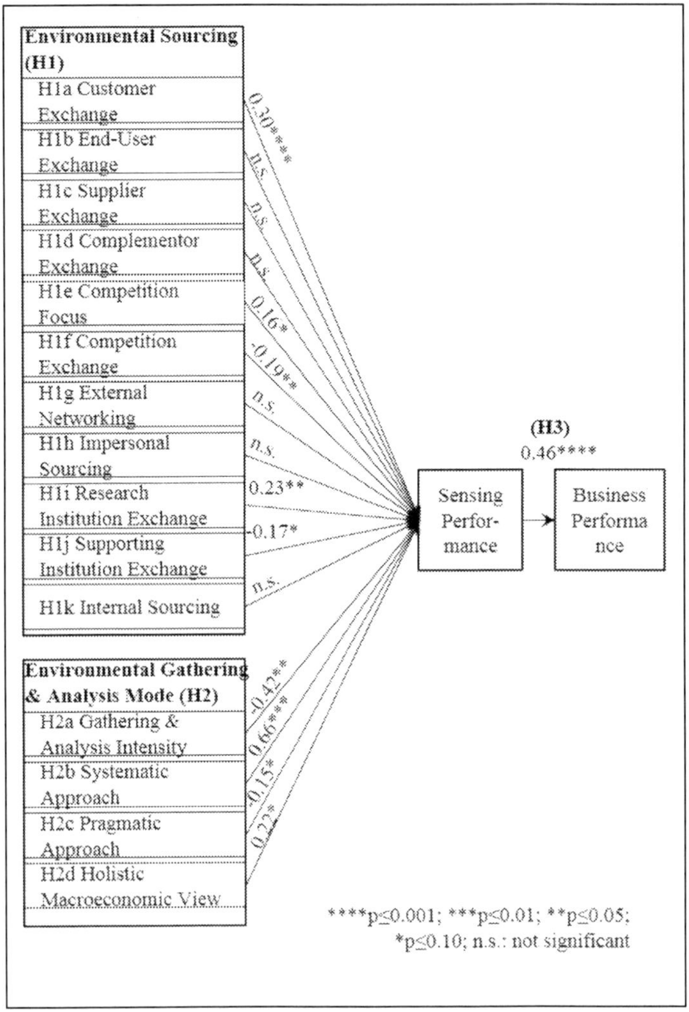

Figure 8 - Structural Equation Modeling Results for High Dynamic Environment (Model 1b)

Then, hypotheses 4a and 4b were verified, which focus on the environmental dynamic impact on the sensing relationships using a multi-group causal analysis, which was similar to the approach of Helm and Landschulze (2013). To test this moderation effect, the data base was divided with a median split (Arbuckle, 2003; Arbuckle & Wothke, 1999) into a low environmental dynamic and a high environmental dynamic section (Model 1b/1c – Figure 9/Figure 10). The comparison of structural effects across the environmental dynamic groups requires that an investigation of the measurement invariance across the single group models can be conducted. For the multi-group causal analysis the same model is just examined under low environmental conditions and under high environmental conditions.

6.2.1.2 Quality Assessment of the Measurement Model – Validity and Reliability Measures

The convergent validity of the multi-item constructs was tested by conducting a principal-axis factor analysis for all exogenous and endogenous variables. The standardized factor loadings exceed the recommended minimum value of 0.4 for all items (Ford, MacCallum, & Tait, 1986). In the next step, a confirmatory factor analysis was performed to finally confirm the validity of the model relations (Jöreskog & Sörbom, 1993).

Cronbach's alpha for all tested constructs is equal to or above the recommended minimum level of 0.7 (Nunally & Bernstein, 1994). The average variance extracted, which should lie above 0.5 (Fornell & Larcker, 1981), or at least above 0.45 (Netemeyer, Bearden, & Sharma, 2003) was also tested. The model also confirmed these criteria. The average variance extracted with the squared correlation between the constructs to test for discriminant validity of the multi-item constructs was compared. The average variance extracted for all constructs tested is greater than the squared correlation, except for the constructs "gathering and analysis intensity" and "systematic approach" (Fornell & Larcker, 1981). A Chi-square difference test on the constructs "gathering and analysis intensity" and "systematic approach," however, resulted in a Chi-square difference value of 38.30, which lies above the required 3.84 (Greenwood & Nikolin, 1996), meaning that both constructs measure different aspects. Altogether, it can be said that the constructs are valid and reliable.

It was also examined whether there was a potential non-response bias by employing a t-test to examine significant differences in the response behavior of early and late respondents, respectively. The reasons for this are that the responses given by late respondents tend to be more like those of non-respondents (Armstrong & Overton, 1977; Jansen, Simsek, & Cao, 2012). However, the t-test results do not show any significant differences between these groups, indicating that non-response bias does not play a role in this study.

6.2.1.3 Quality Assessment of the Structural Equation Model

By using the following recommended indices, the fit of data to the hypotheses from Model 1a and Model 1b/1c was assessed. First, the Chi^2 probability should be above the recommended minimum level of 0.05 (Bagozzi, 1980). Second, the comparative fit index (CFI) should be above or near 0.90 (Barrett, 2007). Third, the cut-off point for the standardized root mean square residual (SRMR) should be below 0.08 (Hu & Bentler, 1999). Finally, the root mean square error of approximation (RMSEA) has to be less than 0.08 (Browne & Cudeck, 1993). Neither the goodness-of-fit index (GFI) nor the adjusted goodness-of-fit index (AGFI) was used, because current simulation studies question the usefulness of these criteria (Sharma et al., 2005). As presented in

Table 4, the above-mentioned model-fit criteria are all met, which means that the models analyzed (Model 1a, Model 1b/1c) are acceptable.

The assessment of the measurement invariance to identify the aspects of inequality for the two environmental dynamic groups held positive results including the differences in the global fit statistics between the restricted and the baseline model/unconstrained models, which have to be smaller than 0.01 (De Jong, Steenkamp, & Fox, 2007). As an analogy to the approach of Helm and Landschulze (2013), the variables and items in both groups need to be the same, which is the case here. Thus, there are no limits on comparing effects between constructs across the two groups. Further, the Chi^2 values significantly increase by imposing equality restrictions on structural weights on top of the restrictions according to configural and metric invariance (Bensaou, Coyne, & Venkatraman, 1999). Using a chi-squared difference test, the comparability of the results for high versus low levels of environmental dynamism (Model 1b and 1c) was further confirmed. Obviously, environmental dynamics moderate the effects between some of the constructs of the model.

Model	**CFI**	**SRMR**	**RMSEA**	**Chi^2**	**d.f.**	**Normed Chi^2**
Model 1a: Overall Sample	0.91	0.06	0.05	699	368	1.9
Model 1b/1c: Subsamples	0.89	0.07	0.03	1.165	736	1.6

Table 4 - Model 1 Statistics

6.2.1.4 Results of Model 1

Figure 8 below reports the results for the overall sample (Model 1a),

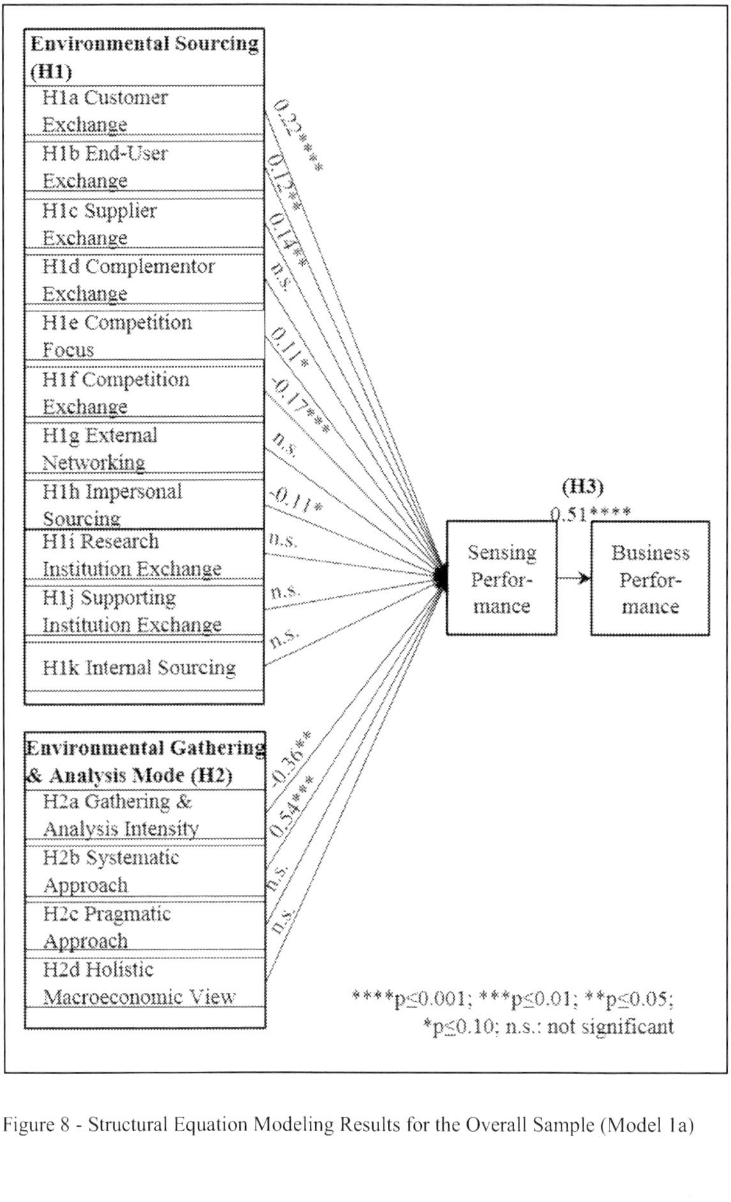

Figure 8 - Structural Equation Modeling Results for the Overall Sample (Model 1a)

while Figure 9 and Figure 10 present the results for the moderating effect of environmental dynamism on the sensing relationships (Model 1b, 1c).

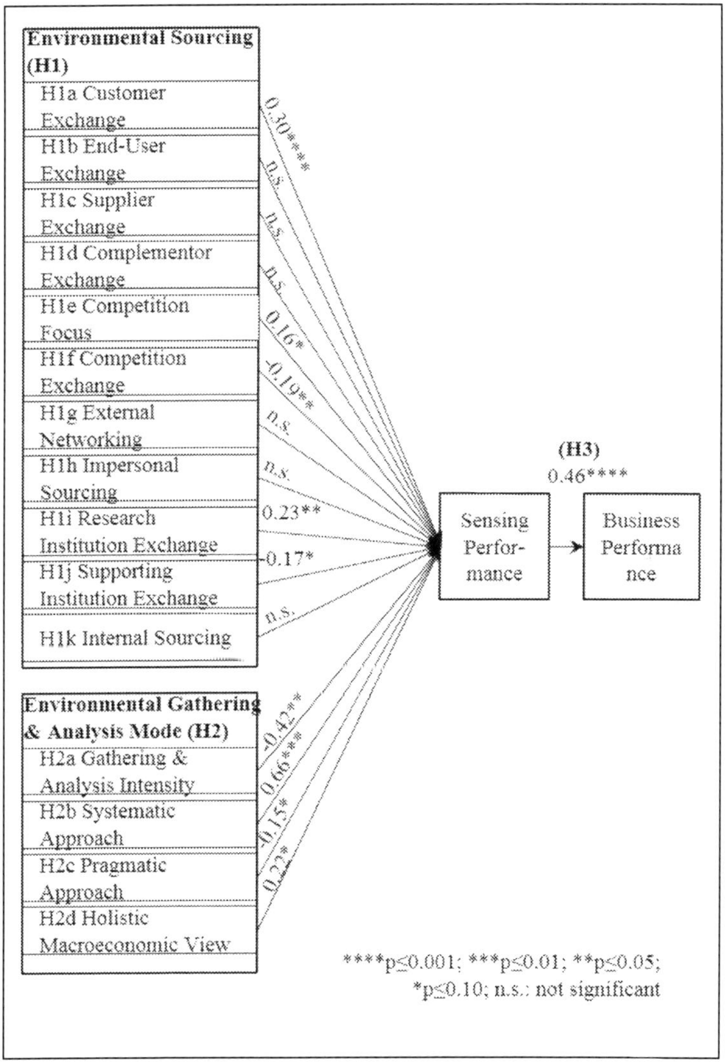

Figure 9 - Structural Equation Modeling Results for High Dynamic Environment (Model 1b)

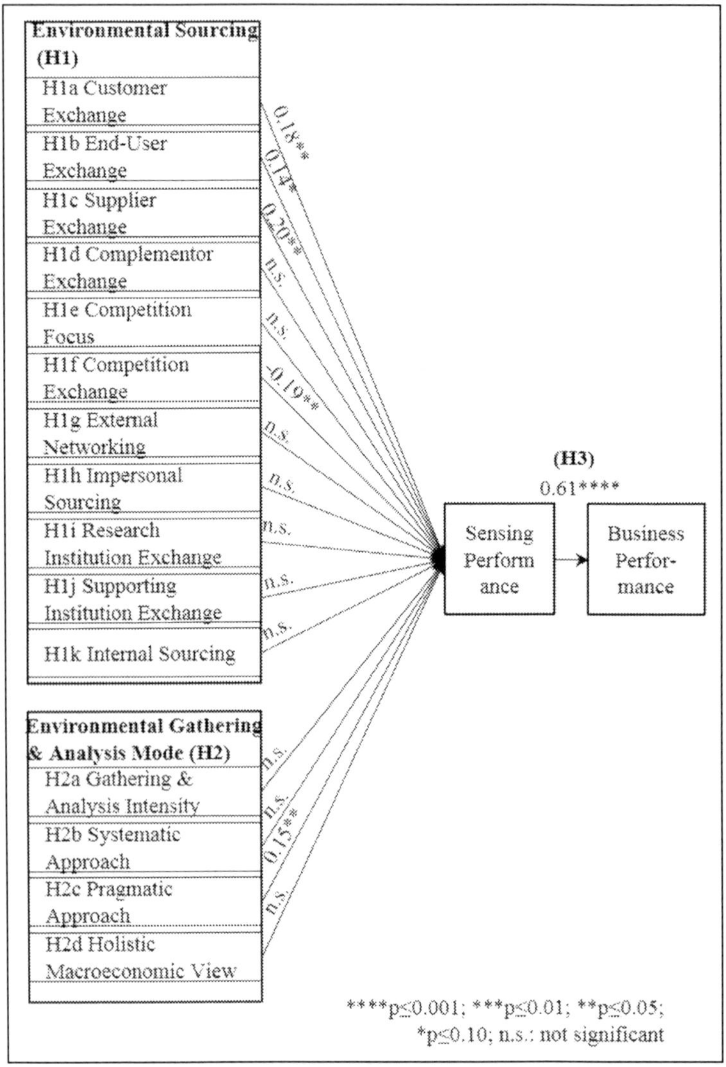

Figure 10 - Structural Equation Modeling Results for Low Dynamic Environment (Model 1c)

Environmental sourcing (H1) has a highly significant effect on the sensing performance. In particular, the exchange with value chain partners (H1a, H1b, H1c) positively drives the sensing performance. While the complementor exchange (H1d), the institutional exchanges (H1i, H1j), the external networking (H1g), and the internal sourcing (H1k) have no significant impact on the sensing performance, competition exchange (H1e), competiton focus (H1f), and impersonal sourcing (H1h) show significant path coefficients to the sensing performance.

As hypothesized on the environmental gathering and analysis mode (H2), a strong positive systematic approach (H2b) can be assessed as a predictor of sensing performance. While the significant strong negative effect of the gathering and analysis intensity contradicts the hypothesis (H2a), the pragmatic approach (H2c), and the holistic macroeconomic view (H2d) cannot be confirmed because of missing significance.

The sensing performance can further be confirmed as a predictor of business performance (H3).

As many research studies have concluded, environmental dynamism has an influence on the sensing relationships. A comparison of Figure 9 with Figure 10 shows that in low dynamic environments, the exchange with all value chain partners, including end-users and suppliers, plays a significant role in achieving sensing performance, while in highly dynamic environments, the sensing performance is primarily predicted by an exchange with the value chain partner customer.

Further, in both environments, competition exchange is negatively related to sensing performance. For the institutional exchange predictors, it was found that in a high dynamic environment, research institution exchange is positively related, and supporting institution exchange is negatively related to sensing performance. The environmental moderating effect makes clear that the gathering and analysis intensity, the systematic approach, and the holistic macroeconomic view are only significantly related to sensing performance in high dynamic environments.

Interestingly, the pragmatic approach has the opposite effect on the sensing performance under different environmental dynamics.

To some extent these results stand in contrast to the hypotheses formulated (H4a, H4b) that environmental dynamism does not just strengthen the relations within the model, but that it partly leads to different effects. In line with Wilhelm, Schlömer, and Maurer's (2015) interpretation of moderating effects of environmental dynamism, it can be said that different effects under high and low environmental dynamism refer to the more extreme environmental conditions (high and low dynamism). Therefore, the results for the relationships under these extreme conditions are allowed to differ and can be accepted next to the hypotheses and results derived from the general sample.

The parameter estimates for the control variables show that there is no significant effect of firm size on the model's relationships; however, the risk-taking has a significant positive impact on the sensing performance of a company. This indicates that companies which are more willing to take risks are able to sense opportunities and threats more easily. This effect is not a focal point of this study, but should nevertheless be taken into consideration, and will be addressed again in Chapter 6.3.

6.2.1.5 Discussion of Model 1

The results of this study provide a holistic and precise picture of the sensing capability. The conceptual and empirical approach to sensing yields several new insights for science and management. Before the concrete implications and insights are discussed, the general contributions of the analysis of Model 1 are given below:

(1) The study of Model 1 delivers a concrete empirical model for one dimension (sensing) of the dynamic capabilities frame, thereby responding to numerous calls for future research that suggested this abstract concept be broken down into

concrete and manageable aspects. To achieve this, measures and constructs were developed to investigate the sensing concept.

(2) By examining concrete environmental sourcings in relation to sensing, information about the impact of specific sources used for gathering environmental information on the sensing of opportunities and threats is delivered. Encompassing all the relevant environmental information sourcing channels, including those of the dynamic capabilities framework, represents a further advance in management research.

(3) Since the sensing activities have been classified into "environmental sourcing", and the "environmental gathering and analysis mode", this study is the first to introduce a concept which integrates both the environmental sources and the way these sources are interpreted. Using this approach, the effects of sources are compared with the effects of the gathering and analysis mode, providing insights into the impact differences between these dimensions of sensing.

(4) The moderating variable environmental dynamism has been included in this study. The sensing relations could thereby be determined for low and high dynamism in the environment, and actually show differences between these two conditions, which means that different mechanisms form the sensing capability in different dynamic environments.

The overall contributions become more tangible when looking at the concrete contributions of the study of Model 1, which will be provided in the following. This begins with insights regarding "sensing performance and business performance", followed by those on "environmental sourcing and sensing performance" and ends with those on the "environmental gathering and analysis mode, and sensing performance". The findings on the moderating effects of environmental dynamism have been included in the respective parts concerned.

Sensing Performance in Relation to Business Performance

In this study, it is proposed that the actual identification of opportunities and threats is directly related to the financial success of companies, because this achievement reflects a good understanding of the market and a quick and effective response to external change, which is the fundament for companies' long-term success (Tseng & Lee, 2014; Yang & Liu, 2012). This was examined, and in terms of the specific results, sensing performance has a strong positive relationship with business performance. This finding supports the argument as hypothesized that the ability to perceive threats and opportunities is a key ingredient for the good financial performance of companies. The rather strong effect of sensing performance on business performance delivers also an answer to prior research discussions if there is a direct or indirect link between dynamic capabilities and organizational outcomes (Eriksson, 2014). The strong positive results between the two constructs sensing performance and business performance further proves that at least sensing, as one dimension of the DCs, positively affects company's performance, and thereby addresses another research gap questioning the positive effect between DCs and organizational outcome which has been automatically assumed in the literature (Eriksson, 2014).

Table 5 highlights the effects of the sensing activities on the sensing performance. This is potentially important because prior research did not focus on sensing activities in conjunction with sensing success, and therefore did not investigate a comprehensive picture of sensing or the sensing capability.

Sensing Activities	Overall	High Dynamism	Low Dynamism
Customer Exchange	+	+	+
End-User Exchange	+	n.s.	+
Supplier Exchange	+	n.s.	+
Competition Focus	+	+	n.s.
Competition Exchange	–	–	–
Impersonal Sourcing	–	n.s.	n.s.
Research Institution Exchange	n.s.	+	n.s.
Supporting Institution Exchange	n.s.	(–)	n.s.
Gathering and Analysis Intensity	(–)	(–)	n.s.
Systematic Approach	+	+	n.s.
Pragmatic Approach	n.s.	–	(+)
Holistic Macroeconomic View	n.s.	+	n.s.

„+" significant positive effect; „-" significant negative effect; „n.s." not significant; "( )" contrary to the hypothesis; All effects are significant at $p \leq 0.10$

Table 5 - Sensing Activities' Effects on Sensing Performance

Environmental Sourcing and Sensing Performance

The results suggest that the exchange with the main value chain partners drives the sensing performance of a company. This is consistent with the findings of Matsuno, Mentzer, and Rentz (2000), who showed the relevance of a value chain partner exchange in relation to market orientiation. By this study's findings, the theory on market orientation can be transferred to a sensing capability theory, making the value chain partner exchange a relevant part of sensing capability. This means that the activity of an *exchange with customers, end-users, and suppliers* positively drives the probability to discover opportunities and threats. By comparing environmental sourcing in the two dynamic contexts, a missing end-user and supplier exchange effect along with a stronger customer exchange effect on the sensing performance in the high dynamic environment can be assessed. As described in the results part above (Chapter 6.2.1.4), it can be concluded that when companies are operating under high levels of environmental dynamism, the only value chain partner that plays a significant role is the customer, while in low dynamic environments all three value chain partners drive the sensing success. This is surprising, since it was assumed that the higher the environmental dynamism, the stronger the respective environmental sourcing impact. This indicates that the sensing capability, and therefore the dynamic capabilities might appear in the form of different activities depending on the level of environmental dynamism, which could be a reason for the DC framework still being abstract and intangible (Barreto, 2010; Eriksson, 2014). One explanation could be that in high dynamic environments the source's end-users and suppliers are too far away from the initial point of change, which is the customer in most cases.

Another contribution emerges from the integration of competitors in the sensing capability construct which suggests that both competition focus and competition exchange play a crucial role in sensing opportunities and threats. First, the effects of competition focus are discussed.

Organizations with increasing levels of *competition focus* increase their level of sensing performance. These findings are consistent with Porter (1980), Kohli and Jaworski (1990), as well as Matsuno, Mentzer, and Rentz (2000), demonstrating that a strong observation of competitors enables companies to anticipate competitors' actions and related market changes more easily, and thereby increases the chances of recognizing opportunities or threats associated with competition. In high dynamic environments, this effect is even stronger, thus suggesting that an orientation toward the competitive environment is even more crucial here.

With respect to this study's specific results, as predicted, *competition exchange* leads to a worse sensing performance. This result was expected but not obvious, since researchers' views on this relationship vary (Hurmelinna-Laukkanen, 2012; Jung-Erceg et al., 2007). As discussed in the previous chapter, on the one hand, the contact to the competition could increase a company's know-how base, and thereby increase the probability of discovering opportunities and threats, but on the other hand, competitors may be reluctant to exchange important information, and maybe even mislead their rivals by providing incorrect information. The negative effect on sensing performance, which also exists in both low and high dynamic environments, further suggests that a market information exchange with rivals should be avoided or at least minimized regarding the successful sensing of a company. It is interesting that no stronger effects of competition exchange have become visible in high dynamic environments, even though it was proposed by authors like Teece, Pisano, and Shuen (1997), or Barreto (2010) that dynamic capabilities might have a higher impact under these conditions. One potential explanation for this might be that the competition exchange is one of the two activities examined, which reduces the sensing performance, and thereby deteriorates a company's sensing capability to conclude that other rules might therefore be applicable.

Looking at the *impersonal sourcing* dimension, the results show another negative relation with the sensing performance, suggesting that Hills and Shrader's (1998) negative media usage effect on opportunity identification could be expanded to an effect on the whole sensing performance, including the identification of threats. This indicates that companies should avoid impersonal sources for collecting market information, as these media could be misleading and not support a company's sensing capability. This finding might be explained by the lack of richness of impersonal sources, which makes it hard for companies to detect subtle signals and business relevant "latent" information in their environment (Daft & Lengel, 1986).

Surprisingly, no significant effect on the sensing of opportunities and threats was found when companies engage in an *internal sourcing* concerning market developments. It was assumed that putting more energy into the internal exchange would increase the likelihood of opportunities or threats being identified. However, looking at the results in retrospect, there may be no relevance for internal sourcing in regard to the actual sensing, perhaps because only information which top management wishes to be heard is actually passed on.

A further contribution stems from insights regarding the institutional exchange concerning developments in the market. In this research, the institutional exchange has no significant impact on the sensing of opportunities and threats under typical environmental conditions. However, looking at companies acting in high dynamic environments, the exchange with institutions is a predictor of sensing performance. Among these, the *supporting institution exchange* has a negative and thereby opposite effect on sensing opportunities and threats in contrast to the *research institution exchange*. This means that the market knowledge generated by the contact with research institutions is relevant for the management of companies in highly dynamic markets to sense opportunities and threats, while an increasing exchange with supporting institutions leads to the identification of fewer opportunities and threats. The negative impact of supporting institutions is quite surprising and was not anticipated in this study, since Teece (2007) suggested considering this source to be able to keep track of the market developments. His line of argument was that supporting institutions like national development institutions promote new technologies or infrastructures such as the expansion of the broadband internet, or innovative ideas and products, and are therefore close to the market. One potential explanation for the consulted negative effect in high dynamic environments might be that these institutions are far behind the fast current developments on the market because of their partly inert and slow-moving administrative machinery, and the lack of an open attitude toward new things within their institutional culture. Therefore, these institutions might be helpful for promoting innovations, and obvious trends which are almost established, but not in regard to finding new business opportunities, or detecting upcoming threats in fast-changing environments. Applying these results to the sensing dimension of the dynamic capabilities framework implies that the sensing capability is mainly driven by the contact between firms and research institutions like universities, while conversations with supporting institutions are rather contraproductive in this respect.

Environmental Gathering and Analysis Mode, and Sensing Performance

The environmental information from the different environmental sources needs to be gathered and then analyzed to sense specific changes in the environment (Teece, 2007; Thomas, Clark, & Gioia, 1993), which automatically begs the question of how to gather and analyze this information. This study also addresses this question by examining the means through which the information on the environment is collected and interpreted. As hypothesized, it is now evident that some environmental gathering and analysis modes have a huge impact on the sensing performance. Moreover, their impact on the sensing of opportunities and threats is stronger than different environmental sourcings. The following discussion of the effects of the respective gathering and analysis modes will give a deeper insight into these effects.

Surprisingly, and contrary to the hypothesis, it was found that companies are less able to sense opportunities and threats using an effortful environmental scanning and interpreting approach (a high *gathering and analysis intensity*). One potential explanation for this unexpected result could be that there is still a difference between "trying" to identify opportunities and threats and the actual identification of them. This assumption would also be supported by Le Meunier-FitzHugh and Piercy (2006), who found that a large number of companies collect information but do not put it to use. Companies which are, for instance, overcommitted to external information search and analysis, and invest a great deal of time and resources in scanning the market might fail to actually perceive opportunities and threats. This phenomenon especially appears in organizations where employees like internal market researchers, or external authorized market research institutes, are only intended to gather and analyze a large amount of information on market developments, but are not intended to draw conclusions in regard to these findings. The task of drawing conclusion in these companies lies with executives who derive their decisions based on an incorrect or incomprehensive understanding of the market situation, as they often do not have much time, or suffer from an information overload, and are therefore not able to fully capture the received market information, so that they fail to sense opportunities and threats effectively. This might especially be the case for larger companies with a more complex organizational structure (Smith, Collins, & Clark, 2005). In such companies it is often the case that the information on market developments is collected by different departments or different persons, such as the key account manager, who only gathers and analyzes the information from the customer. As a consequence, only part, or sometimes none, of the newly generated know-how is forwarded to the executives or the top management, who assess the importance of environmental events and label them as an opportunity or threat for further processing within the company. In line with this argument, there is a lack of effective sharing of market knowledge within the company, which finally prevents companies from actually detecting opportunities and threats, even though a great deal of effort had been put into collecting market data.

A further reason why an intensive mode does not lead to a good sensing performance but more to a bad one could be that the more intensively a company searches, the more specific the search is, as it looks to clarify certain sectors where uncertainty is greatest. Thereby important developments in other market sectors could be overlooked, thus leading to a lower performance in sensing opportunities and threats. This might be caused by specific top management directions or company guidelines which demand a strong focus on specific market sectors.

With respect to the two extremes of environmental dynamism, the results show that the negative gathering and analysis intensity effect becomes visible in high dynamic environments but not in low dynamic environments. This might indicate that companies are overwhelmed by the huge amount of market developments, especially in fast-changing environments, and therefore do not come to concrete conclusions about whether a specific development represents an opportunitiy or a threat, which is actually even more important in high dynamic environments.

To summarize the arguments described, the intensive gathering and analysis of market information negatively affects the actual sensing of opportunities and threats due to the focus on searching being too strong, and the lack of a final conclusion concerning the market information collected. This might be caused by an organizational structure with a division of roles and tasks within the organization, or the lack of time and the information overload in regard to the top management. The most important insight here is that it is more about drawing conclusions from the market screening and analysis than about spending too much time collecting and reviewing market data.

In line with this study's findings on the *systematic gathering and analysis approach*, companies should focus on a method of systematically scanning the environment in order to stay adaptable over time. Those companies that just scan the environment accidentally, or conduct ad hoc analyses of environmental events will sooner or later fail. This includes not only a systematic gathering of data from the environment but also a systematic analysis of this data, which is necessary to reach business-relevant conclusions. Nowadays, many companies have a market intelligence department, which only comes into force at the request of top management. This approach inhibits a constant monitoring of the environment and is mostly concerned with specific market sectors where uncertainty or the knowledge gap, and therefore the "need-to-know" urgency, seem to be the greatest. A continuing procedure ensures the information flow on current market events, and thus a permanent market overview (Helm, Krinner, & Schmalfuß, 2014). By looking at the two extremes of environmental dynamism around companies, an effect of systematic gathering and analysis on the sensing of opportunities becomes visible under high but not low dynamic environments. This might indicate that in environments with a low changing rate, the systematic way is not as important for the identification of opportunities and threats, since the lesser uncertainty in these environments and the lesser complexity often associated with it can also be managed without continuous and structured market information processing, in contrast to high dynamic environments.

By introducing the *pragmatic approach* as an important component of the environmental gathering and analysis mode, the concept of gathering and analyzing information is extended by one aspect. Thus, a more complete conceptualization of sensing is provided which also goes beyond traditional environmental scanning or market information processing concepts (Aguilar, 1967; Daft & Weick, 1984; Flores et al., 2012; Helm, Krinner, & Schmalfuß, 2014; Kohli & Jaworski, 1990; Matsuno, Mentzer, & Rentz, 2000). In addition, empirical evidence is provided to support the importance of the pragmatic approach, thus advancing the literature not only on dynamic capabilities and sensing capability but also on market information processing, market orientation, and environmental scanning. With respect to the specific results of this study, the pragmatic approach cannot be confirmed as a predictor of the sensing of opportunities and threats in the general sample. However, looking at the group division into high and low environmental dynamism, the pragmatic approach has a significantly negative sensing impact for companies in high dynamic environments, and a significantly positive sensing impact for companies in low dynamic environments. On the one hand, the negative impact on the sensing performance under high dynamism indicates that companies in fast-changing environments decrease their opportunity or threat identification rate by using this approach. On the other hand, companies in low dynamic environments increase their sensing outcome by using this approach. These findings show that this practical, solution-oriented method helps companies to discover opportunities and threats in relatively "calm waters". Low dynamic environments promote a less extensive information acquisition and analysis than high dynamic environments, because new market events, such as new technologies or new product offerings, do not come up on a frequent basis where straightforward market information processing would be necessary.

Interestingly, no empirical effects for the *holistic macroeconomic view* in the overall sample were found. Only under high environmental dynamics does the holistic macroeconomic view play a relevant role. Since highly dynamic environments often arise from changes in the macroeconomic environment, such as new regulations or laws, the holistic macroeconomic view seems to be an important success factor there. Moreover, this view helps to get a broad overview of the developments which might affect a firm's business in the future. This could be new regulations in market sectors where the company is not active, as these developments might force the market players there to switch or extend their market activities to business fields of the company in question.

While this study provides a great deal of new insights, like all research it has some limitations, which will be discussed in Chapter 6.3. Despite these limitations, it has shown and proven what sensing or the sensing capability is about, thereby making a significant contribution toward making dynamic capabilities more tangible, and providing concrete activities and measures concerning how to manage environmental change in order to be sustainable as a company.

6.2.2 Model 2 – Environmental Sourcing Differences between Sensing Opportunities and Sensing Threats

6.2.2.1 Data Analysis

A structural equation modeling with maximum likelihood estimation is applied to examine the hypotheses in Model 2. Since the same data set is used to analyze Model 1 and Model 2, multi-normal distribution of the data for Model 2 is assumed to be present, as explained in Chapter 6.2.1.1.

Therefore, the statistical program AMOS (Arbuckle, 2011) is also used, because it is considered superior to traditional statistical methods such as regression analysis or factor analysis, since it is able to measure observed and latent variables simultaneously along with their complex relationships (Shook et al., 2004; Weston & Gore Jr., 2006). Furthermore, the co-variance-based approach to structural equation modeling has been used, since all variables are of reflective nature. The formula from Paternoster et al. (1998) has been used to approve the significance of the hypothesized differences between the effects of the relationships concerned in Model 2.

6.2.2.2 Quality Assessment of the Measurement Model - Validity and Reliability Measures

The validity and reliability of this measurement model can be confirmed in analogy to the quality assessment of Model 1 (see Chapter 6.2.1.2). This can be argued because of the fact that there are no changes in the measurement of environmental sourcing versus the measurement of Model 1 except for the division of the sensing performance into the variables sensing opportunities and sensing threats, which are both measured as single-item constructs.

6.2.2.3 Quality Assessment of the Structural Equation Model

The fit of data with the hypotheses from Model 2 is assessed using the recommended indices as described for Model 1 in Chapter 6.2.1.3. The required model-fit criteria are presented in

Table 6, and are all met, which means that the analyzed Model 2 is acceptable.

Model	**CFI**	**SRMR**	**RMSEA**	**Chi^2**	**d.f.**	**Normed Chi^2**
Model 2	0.92	0.06	0.07	182	68	2.68

Table 6 - Model 2 Statistics

6.2.2.4 Results of Model 2

The results for the overall sample are reported in Figure 11 below. For reasons of clarity, only the significant relationships are illustrated in this figure.

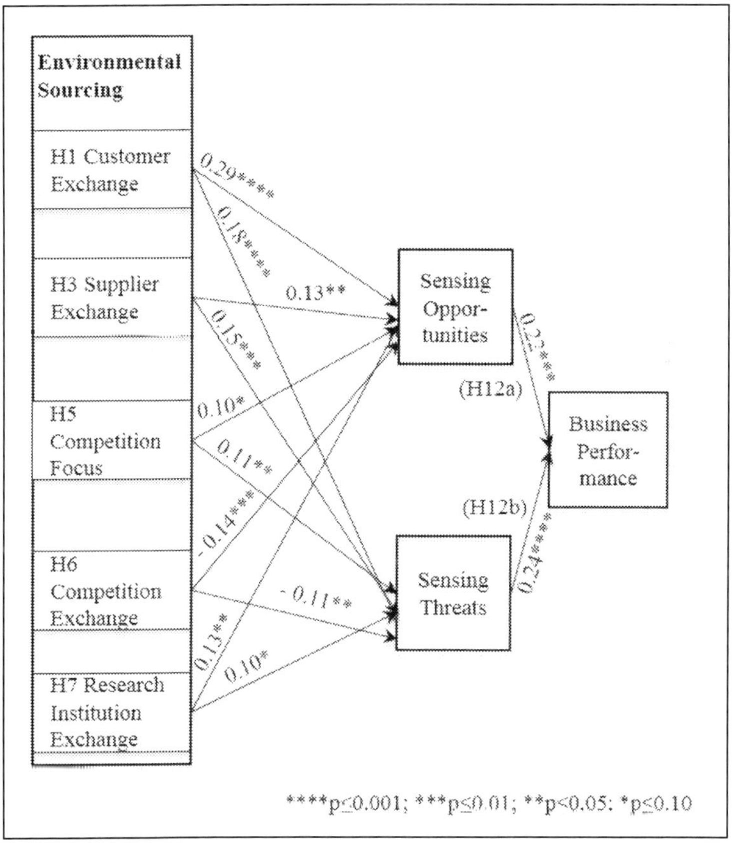

Figure 11 - Significant Results of Model 2

As shown in Figure 11, it is the exchange with customers (H1) in particular that positively drives the sensing of opportunities and threats. By comparing the effects in regard to sensing opportunities and sensing threats respectively, the customer exchange impact on sensing opportunities is much higher than on sensing threats (H1c). While the end-user exchange (H2), the complementor exchange (H4), the supporting institution exchange (H8), the external networking (H9), the internal sourcing (H10), and the impersonal sourcing (H11) show no significant impact either on the sensing of opportunities or on the sensing of threats, competition focus (H5), competition exchange (H6), and research institution exchange (H7) show significant path coefficients to the sensing of opportunities and threats. While competition focus (H5a, H5b) and research institution exchange (H7a, H7b) are positively associated with sensing opportunities and threats, the competition exchange has a negative impact on both sensing opportunities and sensing threats (H6a, H6b). By applying the formula of Paternoster et al. (1998) which was introduced in the data analysis section (Chapter 6.2.2.1), the hypothesized differences between sensing opportunities and sensing threats regarding customer exchange (H1c), competitor exchange (H6c), and research institution exchange (H7c), can only be confirmed to be significant for customer exchange. Further, sensing opportunities and sensing threats can both be confirmed as a predictor of business performance (H12a, H12b). Although the effect that sensing opportunities has on business performance is slightly lower than the effect that sensing threats has on business performance, which would run counter to Hypothesis H12c, no significant difference between the two relationships can be confirmed (Paternoster et al., 1998). As described in the theoretical foundation (Chapter 3.3.2) and hypotheses derivation section (Chapter 4.2.2), no relationships concerning a moderating effect of environmental dynamism were included in Model 2 for reasons of clarity, and no environmental gathering and analysis modes were examined, as there are no theoretical indications of potential differences in the effects on sensing opportunities and the effects on sensing threats.

The parameter estimates for the control variables show that risk-taking has a significant positive effect on the model's relationships, namely on sensing opportunities and sensing threats, but firm size does not. As mentioned for the control variable results of Model 1, this indicates that companies with a higher risk propensity have a greater chance of discovering opportunities and threats. This effect will be addressed again in the section "Limitations" (Chapter 6.3).

6.2.2.5 *Discussion of Model 2*

For this model, the different effects of environmental sourcing on the actual sensing of opportunities or threats were examined. In analyzing the responses of top managers from companies located in Germany, both theory and management practice have been advanced. Before the concrete implications and insights are discussed, the general contributions of the analysis of Model 2 are provided as follows:

(1) By addressing the relationships between environmental sources and two different directions of sensing (sensing opportunities and sensing threats), the study on Model 2 also provides next to Model 1 a deeper understanding of the dynamic capabilities framework. Therefore, this study not only responds to numerous calls for future research that have suggested that this abstract concept of dynamic capabilities should be broken down into concrete and manageable aspects, but also addresses the fact that almost no attention has been paid to the analysis of factors forming the interpretation of market information (Milliken, 1990; O'Reilly, 1982; Sutcliffe, 1997; Vandenbosch, Saatcioglu, & Fay, 2006), especially in regard to potential differences in sensing threats and sensing opportunities (Anderson & Nichols, 2007). Thus, the interesting question which is addressed here is whether the environmental source, or the information from the environmental source, has such a characteristic, therefore tending to have a different effect on whether it is sensed as being an opportunity or a threat.

(2) This study is the first to provide clear and very concrete practical implications for how to use environmental sources for sensing either opportunities or threats. It therefore goes beyond earlier market orientation or environmental scanning research studies, which mainly used these environmental sources as parts of large constructs, and much less for an impact evaluation on sensing opportunities as opposed to sensing threats.

The overall contributions become more tangible when looking at the concrete contributions of the study on Model 2, which will be provided in the following.

Sensing Opportunities and Threats, and Business Performance

Ambiguous research results and theories with respect to the impact of sensing threats and sensing opportunities on companies' business performance have led to calls for further research to figure out whether it is more relevant for companies to sense threats or to sense opportunities (Chattopadhyay, Glick, & Huber, 2001). In terms of the specific results of this study, it was found that both sensing opportunities and sensing threats have a significantly strong positive relationship with business performance. Although the effect of sensing threats is slightly higher than that of sensing opportunities, the application of the formula from Paternoster et al. (1998) shows that this difference is not significant, and is thereby impossible to interpret.

Environmental Sourcing, and Sensing Opportunities and Threats

Table 7 highlights the effects of environmental sourcing on the sensing of opportunities and threats. The results show differences in the importance of various environmental sourcing channels.

Environmental Sourcing	Sensing Opportunities	Sensing Threats
Customer Exchange	++	+
Supplier Exchange	+	+
Competition Focus	+	+
Competition Exchange	–	–
Research Institution Exchange	+	+

"+" positive effect; "-" negative effect; "n.s." not significant; "++" significant stronger positive effect compared to the other dimension of the sensing performance. All effects are significant at $p \leq 0.10$;

Table 7 - Environmental Sourcing Effects on Sensing Opportunities and Threats

The *exchange with customers* plays a key role in companies' sensing of opportunities and threats. Although this is not surprising, the much stronger effect of customer exchange on sensing opportunities as opposed to sensing threats might not have been obvious. This stronger effect can be explained by the fact that many opportunities emerge from customers, and managers tend to keep it in mind to discover business opportunities such as ideas for offering new product solutions while they are speaking with them. This insight is potentially important because prior research has not yet consulted or even examined such an effect to demonstrate that managers should not ignore potential threats in dialog with customers. Moreover, since time and budget is limited within a company, spending too much time on customers might prevent managers or the company from sensing business threats, as the mindset of managers when using this environmental source is focused more on identifying opportunities than on sensing threats.

It should be noted that a significant positive relationship between an *exchange with suppliers* has been found in this study concerning market developments and the sensing of both opportunities and threats. While managers mainly have idea generation or opportunity creation in mind when talking with suppliers, these results show that this exchange can also bear fruit regarding the recognition of threats. This can be explained by the fact that suppliers are well-informed about technological developments or price developments, for example, in order to be able to adapt their technologies on their production sites, or adjust their prices in time. In turn, these developments might pose a risk for their customers, since price increases for suppliers frequently lead to higher prices for the companies supplied, which in turn affects the profit situation of those companies. Therefore, suppliers need to be considered in regard to both sensing opportunities and sensing threats.

In the results of the study, the positive effect of the *competition focus* on both sensing opportunities and sensing threats confirms what Porter (1980) already called for: that competition be observed regularly, no matter whether it is a question of opportunities or threats. The slightly stronger effect of competiton focus on sensing threats than on sensing opportunities might appear logical, since competitors' activities like price reductions or new product offerings can themselves be seen as a threat. However, this difference is not significant (Paternoster et al., 1998).

This study makes another important contribution by clarifying ambiguous research results and reasoning concerning the relevance of *competition exchange* for the identification of opportunities and threats. The results of Model 2 prove that the negative effect of competition exchange on the sensing performance, which was shown in Model 1, is relevant to both the sensing of opportunities and the sensing of threats. This implies that the more intensively the managers of a firm interact with their competition, the fewer opportunities and threats are identified. To prevent this effect, managers and companies should avoid the exchange with competitors concerning market developments. By comparing the impact of competition exchange on sensing opportunities and sensing threats, a greater negative effect on sensing opportunities has been stated, which would mean that even fewer opportunities than threats can be identified using this environmental source. As hypothesized, the source competition features a large perceived uncertainty (Daft, Sormunen, & Parks, 1988), as it is difficult to obtain reliable information from the competition, and according to the threat-rigidity theory where such uncertain issues are viewed favorably as threats, a higher sensing of threats than a sensing of opportunities could be confirmed. Although this reasoning seems logical, and although the theory supports this difference in effect, it has to be considered that this difference is not significant, and cannot therefore be interpreted (Paternoster et al., 1998). A possible focus of future research might be to examine a more differentiated picture (different facets) of competition exchange, thereby perhaps discovering significant effect differences for specific facets of this construct.

With respect to the factor of *"research institution exchange"*, a positive significant effect on the sensing of opportunities and on the sensing of threats was noted. This is quite surprising, since it was predicted that the purpose of research institutions' cooperations, such as the creation of new ideas, would be associated with the sensing of opportunities and not the sensing of threats. However, this assumption was incorrect. One potential explanation for this might be that the exchange with research institutions is not only aimed at the identification of opportunities, but also at the generation of information on general developments or novelties in the market.

While the study of this model provides a great deal of new insights, like all research it has some limitations, which will be discussed in Chapter 6.3. Despite these limitations, the results of Model 2 show factors driving the sensing capability, and, furthermore, factors driving a specific "direction of sensing", meaning either sensing opportunities or sensing threats. The key insight of the investigation of Model 2 is that the type of environmental sourcing does not affect the "direction of sensing", but the effect size between sensing opportunities and sensing threats, at least to some extent. This study makes a further significant contribution toward the understanding of the sensing capability, and therefore of dynamic capabilities, which form the basis of a company's sustainable competitive advantage.

6.3 Research Limitations and Future Research

While this dissertation provides a great number of new insights, like all research, it also has some limitations. The sampling within the manufacturing industries which was used for the analysis of the research questions of this dissertation, means that this study can only be generalized for this sector. To increase the validity of these findings, future studies should either extend the sample to all industries, or at least investigate specific sectors that have been excluded, such as the service industry. This sample used for this study might be also influenced by different industry effects, as it encompasses various manufacturing industries. More strongly regulated industries, for instance, such as the pharmaceutical industries, or industries with oligopolistical structures, meaning fewer competitors, such as the automobile industry, might show variations in the sensing relationships examined. Another limitation of this study is the focus on German companies. If the sensing concept were studied with companies from different nations, like the emerging markets, there might be variations in the relationship between the different sensing activities and the sensing performance, especially in

Chinese companies, where the impact of institutional exchanges, for example, might be higher than for German companies.

Although the control for firm size did not show any significant effects within the models examined, researchers could try to further validate this study's research findings by studying the sensing activities in companies with fewer than 100 employees, as these small companies tend to have less complex organizational structures, and also fewer slack resources, which might affect their sensing behavior. Since there were significant effects of the control variable risk-taking on the model's relationships, implying that a certain risk-propensity of companies affects the sensing performance of a company, future studies might be interested to investigate the lower and higher risk-taking firms as two separate groups by a multi-group causal analysis to test for differences in the effects on the sensing performance. Although potential distortion effects of these variables were controlled for within the empirical model, future studies could further integrate other organizational activities or processes which might interact with the sensing activities and sensing performance, and potentially change or confirm their effects.

Even though the final sample of this study fits to the company size distribution of the original defined statistical population, and a large sample size is given, representativity for German manufacturing companies with more than 100 employees cannot be achieved because of the nature of the random sample wich was used (Bortz, 2006; Von der Lippe & Kladroba, 2002).

Although the survey study conducted has the advantage that the data material can be directly tailored to fit the respective research requests, this research method also has some disadvantages, such as a potential recall bias. A recall bias could lie in the fact that the respondents of this study answer the questions by taking a retrospective view of the activities or performance of their company. Therefore, it has to be taken into account that such estimates are only approximations of reality, as the respondents might have gaps or misperceptions in their memory (Bortz, 2006; Schnell, Hill, & Esser, 2008).

In order to prevent a common-method bias, the suggestions of Podsakoff et al. (2003) have been integrated in this survey's questionnaire. Due to time scarcity, and a current overload of research requests to companies and executives, the decision was made to use the same respondents as a source for both exogenous and endogenous variables. Consequently, a potential common-method bias cannot be definitely excluded (Podsakoff & Organ, 1986; Podsakoff et al., 2003). Nevertheless, using a survey on two different time points on the endogenous variable might be an option for future studies, to ensure the exclusion of common-method variance (Chang, Van Witteloostuijn, & Eden, 2010; Lin & Bhattacherjee, 2009).

This study derived its conclusions for environmental effects on the model from a dichotomous distinction of environmental dynamism. Due to this approach, there were a significant number of companies in each group, which made it possible to run AMOS, and compare both contexts with robust results. However, for future studies, researchers might want to take a more differentiated approach by analyzing different intensities of environmental dynamism in regard to the sensing relationships.

In addressing the sensing capability as one dimension of the dynamic capabilities framework, this part of the framework was rendered more tangible and therefore manageable, further studies could still be done on the other dimensions to finally offer a clear and tangible picture of the whole framework. While this study examined the sensing capability at the firm level and thereby provided valuable insights and implications for companies and their management, future research could further examine this concept at the individual level. Therefore, Teece (2012) has already identified individual capabilities as one microfoundation of the dynamic capabilities framework, and called them "dynamic managerial capabilities". These capabilities could best be analyzed through in-depth qualitative research (e.g. Danneels, 2011), since "the research paradigm of dynamic capabilities is still relatively new", "the empirical literature is still at an early stage", and "opportunities abound to dig deeper into the linkages between individual or small-group managerial actions, dynamic capabilities, and long-run firm performance" (Teece, 2012: 1400).

The limitations mentioned above show that there is a further need to overcome some methodological issues in this study, and to extend the empirical research on this topic. Nevertheless, the conceptualization of sensing as "environmental sourcing", and "environmental gathering and analysis mode", has advanced the dynamic capabilities literature, and provided a specific picture linking concrete sensing activities to sensing performance, which is further associated with business performance. The specific contribution of this study will be described in the next chapter.

7 Overall Summary and Contribution

In this chapter, which is structured in three sections, an overview of the dissertation is given along with the contributions to research and practice. Chapter 7.1 provides an overall summary of the dissertation to illustrate briefly the basic idea behind this research project, the derivation of the concept, the operationalization, the procedure, and the main findings of this study. Chapter 7.2 highlights the contributions of this thesis to research, followed by the practical implications for companies and their management in Chapter 7.3 and some concluding remarks in Chapter 7.4.

7.1 Summary of the Dissertation

The increasing speed in the business environment is leading to new challenges in the management of companies. Adaptability is increasingly becoming a competitive advantage for companies, as typical competitive advantages become more and more temporary in nature (McNamara, Valler, & Devers, 2003; Wiggins & Ruefli, 2005). While earlier approaches like behavioral theory, contingency theory, and even Porter's Five Forces or the RBV have revealed weaknesses in regard to the management of constant changes in the business environment, the dynamic capabilities approach provides a sound answer to this issue.

Many studies have been conducted on dynamic capabilities, but the research has remained rather superficial, with no real tangible or concrete activities behind the dynamic capabilities framework being given (Barreto, 2010; Eriksson, 2014). This provides the research gap of "making dynamic capabilities more tangible", which is the focus of this dissertation. The difficulty, however, is where to start.

According to Protogerou, Caloghirou, and Lioukas (2012), and Teece (2007), sensing seems to be the most relevant dimension of the dynamic capabilities framework, since it provides the basis for the other dimensions of "seizing", "learning", "managing threats and reconfiguration", and "monitoring" in this framework. In view of this and the research gap mentioned above, the essential goal of this dissertation is to make the sensing capability more tangible. Therefore, a concept based on Aguilar (1967), Daft and Weick (1984), and Teece (2007) was developed, which divides the sensing capability into sensing activities, and sensing performance, whereby sensing activities are further divided into environmental sourcing, and the environmental gathering and analysis mode.

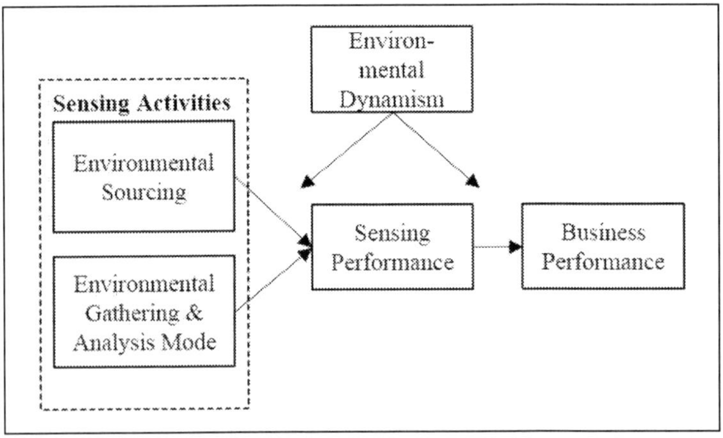

Figure 12 - The Sensing Capability Concept

Based on this concept, which is illustrated in Figure 12, the model was operationalized primarily with the help of Matsuno, Mentzer, and Rentz (2000), Barney (1995), Teece (2007), and Flores et al. (2012), and was thereby rendered measurable. In order to gain a holistic view, and to ensure true relevance for the company or the management of the company, the sensing performance has also been set in relation to the business performance. Furthermore, since several studies on dynamic capabilities have integrated different kinds of dynamism in their models, some of them with ambiguous results, the decision was made to integrate environmental dynamism in the study as well. Thus, this study is able to show differences

in sensing under low and high environmental dynamism. In addition to the specification of sensing, the following question is raised: whether environmental sourcing as part of the sensing activities might differ regarding its effect on sensing opportunities as opposed to sensing threats. This is addressed in this study using a separate model (Model 2).
After having conducted interviews with corporate executives from 10 different small and large manufacturing companies, the questionnaire for the online survey with academic research experts and top managers was pretested. The conclusions drawn from this had been included in an online survey with the top management of German companies, which were then analyzed with AMOS based on a structural equation model. The analysis shows which environmental sourcing, and which environmental gathering and analysis mode activities have an impact on the actual sensing of opportunities and threats under different environmental dynamics (Model 1), and which environmental sourcing activities have different effects on the sensing of opportunities as opposed to the sensing of threats (Model 2).

First of all, the sensing performance was assessed as having a strong positive impact on the business performance, showing its high relevance for companies. A further effect identified was that specific gathering and analysis modes have a much stronger influence on the sensing of opportunities and threats than any environmental sourcings. Besides the insight that an exchange with typical value chain partners like customers or suppliers leads to a positive sensing performance, it was assessed that an exchange with competitors is negatively related to the actual sensing of opportunities and threats. Regarding the environmental gathering and analysis mode, it was quite surprising that the intensity of gathering and analyzing environmental information has a negative effect on the sensing of opportunities and threats, while the systematic gathering and analysis mode has a strong positive effect on it. The concrete contributions of these and the following findings will be explained in detail in Chapter 7.2 and Chapter 7.3.

The division of the data set into the two groups "high dynamic environment" and "low dynamic environment" showed that there are differences concerning the effects, and the extent of the effects. Most interesting here are the following three findings. First, the negative impact of the intensity of environmental gathering and analysis, and second, the positive impact of a systematic approach to gathering and analyzing environmental information on the sensing performance only showed up in the high dynamic environment. Third, the pragmatic approach was positively correlated with the sensing performance under low dynamic environments, while a negative impact of this relationship showed up in high dynamic environments. It can therefore be concluded that the sensing capability appears in the form of different activities depending on the environmental dynamism. Along with these results, this dissertation brought out some interesting insights concerning environmental sourcing, and its impact on sensing opportunities as opposed to sensing threats (Model 2). The main finding to emerge from the examination of Model 2 is that there are no differences in the effect direction, meaning that there is not a negative relation of an environmental sourcing activity on sensing opportunities, whilst sensing threats is positively affected by this activity. It was further shown that while the environmental sources supplier exchange, research institution exchange, and competitor exchange have almost the same effect on both sensing opportunities and sensing threats, the source customer exchange has a much higher impact on sensing opportunities than on sensing threats, meaning that companies' dialog with customers primarily increases the opportunity rate. What is rather surprising about these findings is that except for the customer exchange, there are no significant differences between the effect sizes of environmental sourcings on sensing opportunities as opposed to sensing threats, unlike what was predicted by the theory.

This dissertation provides a large number of new insights. The results show which aspects form the sensing capability in general, and how the sensing capability appears in low and high dynamic environments. In this study it was shown and proven what sensing is about, and that there are differences between sensing opportunities and sensing threats, thus providing a significant contribution to making both dynamic capabilities and the way to achieve sustainable competitive advantages more tangible.

7.2 *Research Contribution*

In addressing the main research questions from Chapter 1.4, this dissertation makes an important contribution to research, as described in the following:

(1) It delivers a concrete empirical model for one dimension (sensing) of the dynamic capabilities framework, thereby responding to numerous calls for future research which suggested that this abstract concept be broken down into concrete and manageable aspects. To achieve this, measures and constructs were developed to investigate the sensing concept by integrating different theoretical concepts and research results (strategic management, marketing, entrepreneurship, organizational science) under the heading of sensing. In addition, given that there are only few quantitative studies on the elements of DCs (Eriksson, 2014), it was worth developing measures that were used to quantify the phenomenon, and which might be applicable for future empirical research into DCs.

(2) By examining concrete environmental sourcings in relation to sensing, this dissertation is the first study to deliver information about the impact of specific sources used for gathering environmental information on the sensing of opportunities and threats. Encompassing all the relevant environmental information sourcing channels, including those of the dynamic capabilities theory, represents a further advance in management research. This surpasses earlier research on market orientation or environmental scanning, which mainly uses environmental sources as part of large constructs, such as the "Intelligence Generation" construct by Kohli, Jaworski, and Kumar (1993), and therefore gives no specific answers concerning the effects of the different environmental sources.

(3) Since the sensing activities have been classified into "environmental sourcing", and the "environmental gathering and analysis mode", this study is the first to introduce a concept which integrates both the environmental sources and the way these sources are interpreted. Using this approach, the effects of the various sources can be compared with the effects of the gathering and analysis modes, providing insights into impact differences. Thereby, it was shown that the environmental gathering and analysis modes "gathering and analysis intensity" as

well as the "systematic approach" have a greater impact on the successful sensing of opportunities and threats than a company's exchange with any environmental source.

(4) "The mechanisms by which dynamic capabilities lead to performance outcomes were found to be an unresolved issue in empirical research" (Eriksson, 2014: 65). Following this research call, this study identified mechanisms in the form of concrete sensing activities in relation to their performance, and their impact on a company's outcome in terms of business performance. By examining the linkage between sensing performance and business performance, this study goes beyond prior research (Barreto, 2010; Eriksson, 2014), as it proves that a direct, and not an indirect, link between sensing and the business performance exists. This finding supports the argument as hypothesized that the ability to perceive threats and opportunities is a key ingredient for the good financial performance of companies. Although this result can only be found to be valid for the sensing dimension of the DCs, this study thus delivers a further contribution to research, as it examines a concrete dimension (sensing) of the dynamic capabilities framework, in contrast to earlier research (e.g. Wu, 2007; Zhang, 2007), which investigated the relationship between the whole dynamic capability framework and a company's performance. The positive relationship found between sensing performance and business performance confirms the hypothesis that the actual identification of opportunities and threats, meaning an effective sensing capability, promotes the financial success of companies, and therefore addresses another research gap which questions the positive effect between DCs and organizational outcome that is automatically assumed by researchers (Eriksson, 2014). To sum up, the sensing capability is a crucial success factor for companies.

(5) In Model 2, the relationship between sensing performance and business performance was also examined. However, here the sensing performance was divided into the two parts sensing opportunities and sensing threats. In accordance with the prospect theory (Kahnemann & Tversky, 1979; Tversky & Kahnemann, 1986; White, Varadarajan, & Dacin, 2003), and the threat-rigidity theory (Ocasio, 1995; Staw, Sandelands, & Dutton, 1981), it was assumed that there might be differences

between the effect of sensing opportunities and the effect of sensing threats on a company's business performance. A further research contribution is provided by this study purely by the development and testing of this hypothesis. Interestingly, the results show small but insignificant differences between the impact of sensing opportunities and sensing threats on business performance. This might indicate that this relation should be regarded in a more differentiated way by future research in order to figure out what specific aspects might drive a significant difference between these impacts, maybe with the help of illuminating case studies.

(6) In accordance with research suggestions that high and low environmental dynamics have different effects on dynamic capabilities (Danneels, 2008; Eisenhardt & Martin, 2000; Helfat et al., 2007; Teece, Pisano, & Shuen, 1997), the moderating variable environmental dynamism has been included in this study. The sensing relations were therefore determined for low and high dynamism in the environment, and actually show differences between these two conditions. This provides a further key insight: namely, that sensing capability appears differently depending on the level of environmental dynamism. This becomes visible in the effects of the end-user and the supplier exchange on the sensing performance, for instance, which only appears in a low dynamic environment. This revolutionizes the original idea that there might only be one single specific set of activities forming the sensing capability (Barreto, 2010), and therefore also the dynamic capabilities.

(7) Almost no attention has been paid to the analysis of factors driving or forming the interpretation of market information in prior research (Milliken, 1990; O'Reilly, 1982; Sutcliffe, 1997; Vandenbosch, Saatcioglu, & Fay, 2006), especially in regard to potential differences between sensing threats and sensing opportunities (Anderson & Nichols, 2007). This issue has been addressed in this thesis by looking at various environmental information sources, and their different effects on the sensing of threats as opposed to the sensing of opportunities. Here, it was shown how the perception of a piece of environmental information from a specific environmental source affects the interpretation of it more as an opportunity or a threat. The results show that there are no contradictory effects of

an exchange with environmental sources on the sensing of opportunities as opposed to the sensing of threats. This insight is potentially important because prior research has not begged and empirically examined the question of potential sensing direction differences, which can now be answered. This finding indicates that no matter what kind of environmental sourcing is practiced, the recognition of opportunities and threats is affected concurrently. So there is no need to fear that practicing a certain environmental source might increase the opportunities identified on the one side and diminish the threat identification outcome on the other side. The only significant difference which emerges from this comparison is in the effect of the environmental source "customer", as the impact of it is higher on sensing opportunities than on sensing threats. This insight is also new to research, and indicates that this source tends to produce a higher opportunity identification rate than for threats, as it is very much associated with information richness and the purpose of idea generation.

7.3 *Implications for Practice*

The conceptualization and specification of the sensing capability with its two dimensions and concrete activities provides organizational leaders with a valuable framework to manage the sensing capability, and therefore the adaptability and sustainability of their companies. The concrete practical implications based on the examination of this concept in this dissertation are provided in the following:

(1) Insights derived from studying various environmental information sources and their different effects on the sensing of opportunities and threats will provide a guide for management to focus their attention on the right environmental sourcing activities, depending on the circumstances, and the goals of the company. This is essential, since huge amounts of budget and time are spent on generating or buying market information, and companies often fail to transfer and transform this information effectively (Flores et al., 2012). According to the findings of this study, customer exchange, supplier exchange, end-user exchange, and competition

focus are crucial sourcings. This indicates that companies should focus on meetings or conversations with their customers, suppliers, and end-users to increase their sensing success. As far as customer and end-user sourcing are concerned, firms might thereby disover new trends, changing customer needs, new upcoming target market segments, and ideas for product or process innovations (Teece, 2007). By an intense exchange with suppliers, companies might already recognize innovations of their suppliers at an early stage, receive information about any technological developments in the market, and gain insights by considering a supplier-specific perspective of the market. Besides the exchange with the value chain partners, the findings of this study show that there is also a need to focus on competitors' activities. Monitoring their activities regarding new market developments like new customer trends or new market regulations might particularly help organizational leaders to react to their competitors' movements in time, so that potential threats like new products or price reductions can be recognized early. Since there is not a single environmental sourcing impact, multiple information sourcing can be recommended as a solution to stay informed about the environment, and to detect opportunities and threats, as each environmental sourcing delivers specific, filtered information on market developments, thereby enriching the company's market information base.

(2) As mentioned in the research contribution part, the effects of environmental sourcings on the sensing performance are not only positive; there are also negative effects like the competition exchange and impersonal sourcing. In line with these findings, there is a clear recommendation to minimize the direct exchange with competition or the usage of impersonal sourcings regarding their sensing effect. As was described extensively in Chapter 4.2 on hypotheses derivation, management should avoid conversations with their rivals on market developments, since the information received might be incorrect and misleading. Further, companies should spend less time scanning and analysing diverse media (impersonal sourcing), because there might be too much irrelevant information, which may result in an incorrect assessment of environmental developments, or an opportunity being missed because it was not the first identifier.

(3) By looking at the extremes of environmental dynamism, some differences in the effects of environmental sourcings and in the environmental gathering and analysis mode appeared as mentioned. This is particularly relevant for the management, since different sourcings should be used, or should at least be used with a different intensity, depending on the environmental dynamism in which the company or the respective business unit is operating. The fact that of the value chain partners, only the customer exchange plays a significant role in sensing opportunities and threats in high dynamic environments might especially indicate that the focus of companies' top management in such environments should be on meetings and dialog with them. In contrast, an exchange with end-users and suppliers seems to play a larger role in sensing in low dynamic environments. In addition, the significant effects of competition focus in high dynamic environments, and the lack of effect in low dynamic environments might mean that companies which operate in fast-changing environments should pay special attention to competitors' activities. It is also important to note that all recommendations given in regard to environmental sourcing affect not only the top management of a company but also all departments dealing with these external partners.

(4) Surprisingly, it was found that companies are less able to sense opportunities and threats if they use an intensive environmental scanning and interpreting approach. As discussed in Chapter 6.2.1.5, this result could be explained by a potential difference between "trying" to identify opportunities and threats, and actually identifying them. Thus, when companies are overcommitted to an external information search and analysis, they may still be unable to perceive opportunities and threats. Perhaps the most important insight for management practice here is that it is more about drawing conclusions from the market screening and analysis than about spending too much time reviewing market data. The results of this study also show that this effect only becomes visible in a highly dynamic environment, which could mean that it is mainly companies operating in highly dynamic environments like emerging markets or the IT industry which have to make sure that they do not spend too much time gathering and analyzing environmental

information. For these companies particularly, it is more important to put into practice the information on developments in the market which has been gathered and analyzed. A further factor which might influence the negative effect of intensive gathering and analyzing of market information on the sensing performance could lie in a lack of interfunctional or interdepartmental coordination within the company (Helm, Krinner, & Schmalfuß, 2014; Narver & Slater, 1990). Assuming that different departments within a company scan and analyse the market heavily, and do not exchange the collected information within the company, it may happen that those (e.g. the market research department) who have to conclude whether this market information is an opportunity or a threat do not receive the information or only receive part of it, and hence opportunities or threats might be overlooked. This can be improved by a firm's management by fostering the collaboration between the marketing and sales department, for instance, because both departments are in charge of collecting and analyzing market information (Helm, Krinner, & Schmalfuß, 2014; Kotler, Rackham, & Krishnaswamy, 2006).

(5) In line with the findings concerning the systematic gathering and analysis approach, companies should focus on a method of systematically scanning the environment in order to sense opportunities or threats, and thereby remain adaptable over time. Those companies that only scan the environment accidentally, or conduct ad hoc analyses of environmental events, will fail sooner or later. As these findings show, successful sensing not only involves a systematic gathering of data from the environment, but also a systematic analysis of this data, which is necessary for those responsible in a company to reach conclusions that are relevant to business. Nowadays, many companies have a market intelligence department, which only comes into force at the request of top management. According to the positive relationship of the systematic gathering and analysis of market information and sensing performance which was revealed in this study, the request-oriented behavior of some market intelligence departments should be avoided, as this behavior inhibits the constant monitoring of the environment, and hence the continuous flow of market information, which might lead to

opportunities or threats being overlooked (Le Bon & Merunka, 2006). A systematic approach can be implemented by means of a standardized in-house process for gathering, analyzing, and making decisions based on market information. This approach should be supported or directed by the company's formulated strategy, as this can serve as an attention filter so that not every item of information gathered is interpreted as a potential threat or opportunity, but only those associated with the strategy.

(6) The findings on the pragmatic approach show that while companies in high dynamic environments should avoid this approach, companies in low dynamic environments should use it to be able to sense opportunities and threats. This pragmatic approach is hard to install as a process, as it rather depends on the experience and attitudes of the people responsible for dealing with market information; however, companies can hold training courses, or hire the right people with the right mindset to foster this thinking and acting in regard to the collection and analysis of environmental information.

(7) As was already mentioned in the research contribution part, the results of Model 2 show that there are no contradictory effects of the environmental sourcings on the sensing of opportunities as opposed to the sensing of threats. This finding is good for the management to know, so that they can pay attention to information on both potential threats and potential opportunities in the exchange with every source. The only difference to consider is the effect size difference of the customer exchange. Here, firms tends to recognize more opportunities than threats by practicing this exchange. Since time and budget are limited within a company, spending too much time on customers might lead to a disproportionate recognition of opportunities compared to threats to the business. Therefore, a certain conciousness of this effect is necessary in interactions with customers (Cyert & March, 1963).

7.4 Concluding Remarks

This dissertation contributes a great number of new findings to the research on dynamic capabilities, showing which aspects form the sensing capability in general, and also how it appears in low and high dynamic environments. This study succeeds in making both dynamic capabilities and the way to achieve sustainable competitive advantages more tangible, reveals that there are differences between sensing opportunities and sensing threats, and empirically proves what sensing is about. These insights not only advance the research on dynamic capabilities, but also the research on market orientation and environmental scanning, and provide valuable implications for practice. Therefore, companies and their management are now in a better position to handle adaptability, and generate or hold sustainable competitive advantages.

References

Aguilar, F. J. 1967. ***Scanning the Business Environment***. New York: Macmillan.

Ali, S., Peters, L., & Lettice, F. 2012. An organizational learning perspective on conceptualizing dynamic and substantive capabilities. ***Journal of Strategic Marketing***, 20(7): 589-607.

Ambrosini, V., & Bowman, C. 2009. What are dynamic capabilities and are they a useful construct in strategic management? ***International Journal of Management Reviews***, 11: 29-49.

Ambrosini, V., Bowman, C., & Collier, N. 2009. Dynamic Capabilities: An Exploration of How Firms Renew their Resource Base. ***British Journal of Management***, 20: 9-24.

Anand, G., & Ward, P. T. 2004. Fit, flexibility and performance in manufacturing: coping with dynamic environments. ***Production and Operations Management***, 13: 369-385.

Anderson, M. H. 2008. Social networks and the cognitive motivation to realize network opportunities: a study of managers' information gathering behaviors. ***Journal of Organizational Behavior***, 29 (1), 51-78.

Anderson, M. H., & Nichols, M. L. 2007. Information gathering and changes in threat and opportunity perceptions. ***Journal of Management Studies***, 44: 367-387.

Aragon-Correa, J. A., & Sharma, S. 2003. A contingent resource-based view of proactive corporate environmental strategy. ***Academy of Management Review***, *28*(1): 71-88.

Arbuckle, J. L., & Wothke, W. 1999. ***Amos 4.0 User's Guide***. Chicago: SPSS.

Arbuckle, J. L. 2003. ***Amos 5 User's Guide***. Chicago: SPSS.

Arbuckle, J. L. 2011. ***AmosTM 20 User's Guide***. Chicago.

Arend, R. J., & Bromiley, P. 2009. Assessing the dynamic capabilities view: spare change, everyone? ***Strategic Organization***, 7(1): 75-90.

Armstrong, J. S., & Overton, T. S. 1977. Estimating nonresponse bias in mail surveys. ***Journal of Marketing Research***, 14: 396-402.

Ahuja, H.L. 2007. ***Advanced Economic Theory: Microeconomic Analysis.*** Delhi: S. Chand & Company.

Argyris, C., & Schön, D. A. 1978. ***Organizational Learning: A Theory of Action Perspective***. Reading, MA: Addison-Wesley.

Athreye, S., Kale, D., & Ramani, S. V. 2009. Experimentation with strategy and the evolution of dynamic capability in the Indian pharmaceutical sector. ***Industrial and Corporate Change***, 18(4): 1229-1260.

Atteslander, P. 1984. ***Methoden der empirischen Sozialforschung***. Berlin, New York: Walter de Gruyter.

Augier, M., & Teece, D. J. 2009. Dynamic Capabilities and the Role of Managers in Business Strategy and Economic Performance. ***Organization Science***, 20(2): 410-421.

Auster, E., & Choo, C. W. 1993. Environmental scanning by CEOs in two Canadian industries. ***Journal of the American Society for Information Science***, 44(4): 194-203.

Auster, E., & Choo, C. W. 1994. How senior managers acquire and use information in environmental scanning. ***Information Processing & Management***, 30 (5): 607-618.

Backhaus, K., Erichson, B., Plinke, W., & Weiber, R. 2011. ***Multivariate Analysemethoden. Eine anwendungsorientierte Einführung***. Berlin, Heidelberg: Springer-Verlag.

Backhaus, K., Erichson, B., & Weiber, R. 2013. ***Fortgeschrittene Multivariate Analysemethoden. Eine anwendungsorientierte Einführung***, 2. Edition. Berlin Heidelberg: Springer-Verlag.

Backhaus, K., & Weiber, R. 2007. Forschungsmethoden der Datenauswertung. ***Handwörterbuch der Betriebswirtschaft***, 6: 524-535.

Bagozzi, R. P. 1980. ***Causal models in marketing***. New York: Wiley.

Bagozzi, R. P., & Fornell, C. 1982. Theoretical concepts, measurements, and meaning. ***A second generation of multivariate analysis***, 2(2): 5-23.

Barney, J. B. 1986. Strategic factor markets: Expectations, luck, and business strategy. ***Management Science***, 32(10): 1231-1241.

Barney, J. 1991. Firm resources and sustained competitive advantage. ***Journal of Management***, 17(1): 99-120.

Barney, J. 1995. Looking inside for competitive advantage. ***Academy of Management Executive***, 9(4): 49-61.

Baron, R. A. 2006. Opportunity recognition as pattern recognition: How entrepreneurs "connect the dots" to identify new business opportunities. ***Academy of Management Perspectives***, 20(1): 104–119.

Barr, P. S. 1998. Adapting to unfamiliar environmental events: a look at the evolution of interpretation and its role in strategic change. ***Organization Science***, 9(6): 644-669.

Barr, P. S., Stimpert, J. L., & Huff, A. S. 1992. Cognitive change, strategic action, and organizational renewal. ***Strategic Management Journal***, 13(S1): 15-36.

Barr, P. S., & Glynn, M. A. 2004. Cultural variations in strategic issue interpretation: Relating cultural uncertainty avoidance to controllability in discriminating threat and opportunity. ***Strategic Management Journal***, 25(1): 59-67.

Barreto, I. 2010. Dynamic capabilities: A review of past research and an agenda for the future. ***Journal of Management***, 36(1): 256-280.

Barrett, P. 2007. Structural equation modeling: Adjudging model fit. ***Personality and Individual Differences***, 42(5): 815-824.

Baum, J. R., & Wally, S. 2003. Strategic decision speed and firm performance. ***Strategic Management Journal,*** 24(11): 1107–1129.

Benner, M. J., & Tushman, M. L. 2003. Exploitation, exploration, and process management: The productivity dilemma revisited. ***Academy of Management Review***, 28(2): 238-256.

Bensaou, M., Coyne, M., & Venkatraman, N. 1999. Testing metric equivalence in cross national strategy research: An empirical test across the United States and Japan. ***Strategic Management Journal,*** 20(7): 671-689.

Billings, R. S., Milburn, T. W., & Schaalman, M. L. 1980. A model of crisis perception: A theoretical and empirical analysis. ***Administrative Science Quarterly***, 25(2): 300-316.

Bingham, C., Heimeriks, K., Schijven, M., & Gates, S. 2015. Concurrent learning: How firms develop multiple dynamic capabilities in parallel. ***Strategic Management Journal***, early view.

Blalock, H. M. 1964. ***Causal inferences in nonexperimental research***. Chapel Hill: University of North Carolina Press.

Blyler, M., & Coff, R. W. 2003. Dynamic capabilities, social capital, and rent appropriation: Ties that split pies. ***Strategic Management Journal***, 24(7): 677-686.

Bollen, K. A. 1989. ***Structural Equations with Latent Variables***. New York: Wiley.

Bortz, J. 2006. ***Statistik: Für Human-und Sozialwissenschaftler***. Heidelberg: Springer Medizin Verlag.

Brenner, M. J. 2009. Dynamic or Static Capabilities? Process Management Practices and Response to Technological Change. ***Journal of Product Innovation Management***, 26(5): 473-486.

Brown, S. L., & Eisenhardt, K. M. 1998. ***Competing on the edge: Strategy as structured chaos***. Cambridge, MA: Harvard Business Press.

Brown, M. W. 1982. Covariance Structures, in: Hawkins, D. M. (Ed.): ***Topics in Applied Multivariate Analysis***, Cambridge, 72-141.

Browne, M. W., & Cudeck, R. 1993. Alternative ways of assessing model fit. ***Sociological Methods & Research***, 21(2): 230-258.

Burns, T. E., & Stalker, G. M. 1961. ***The management of innovation***. University of Illinois at Urbana-Champaign's Academy for Entrepreneurial Leadership Historical Research Reference in Entrepreneurship.

Cantor, N., Mischel, W., & Schwartz, J. C. 1982. A prototype analysis of psychological situations. ***Cognitive Psychology***, 14(1): 45-77.

Cavusgil, S. T., Calantone, R. J., & Zhao, Y. 2003. Tacit knowledge transfer and firm innovation capability. ***Journal of Business & Industrial Marketing***, 18(1): 6-21.

Chandler, A. D. 1990. The enduring logic of industrial success. ***Harvard Business Review***, 68(2): 130-140.

Chang, S. J., Van Witteloostuijn, A., & Eden, L. 2010. Common method variance in international business research. ***Journal of International Business Studies***, 41(2): 178-184.

Chattopadhyay, P., Glick, W. H., & Huber, G. P. 2001. Organizational actions in response to threats and opportunities. ***Academy of Management Journal***, 44(5): 937-955.

Chen, C. L., & Jaw, Y. L. 2009. Building global dynamic capabilities through innovation: A case study of Taiwan's cultural organizations. ***Journal of Engineering and Technology Management***, 26(4): 247-263.

Child, J. 1972. Organizational structure, environment and performance: The role of strategic choice. ***Sociology***, 6(1): 1-22.

Child, J. 1997. Strategic choice in the analysis of action, structure, organizations and environment: retrospect and prospect. ***Organization Science***, 18: 3- 76.

Churchill Jr, G. A. 1979. A paradigm for developing better measures of marketing constructs. ***Journal of Marketing Research***, 16(1): 64-73.

Collis, D. J. 1994. How valuable are organizational capabilities? ***Strategic Management Journal***, 15(special issue): 143-152.

Cross, R., & Sproull, L. 2004. More than an answer: Information relationships for actionable knowledge. ***Organization Science***, 15(4): 446-462.

Cyert, R. M., & March, J. G. 1963. ***A Behavioral Theory of the Firm***. Englewood Cliffs, NJ: Prentice-Hall.

Daft, R. L., & Lengel, R. H. 1986. Organizational information requirements, media richness and structural design. ***Management Science,*** 32(5): 554-571.

Daft, R. L., & Sormunen, J., & Parks, D. 1988. Chief executive scanning, environmental characteristics, and company performance: An empirical study. ***Strategic Management Journal,*** 9(2): 123-139.

Daft, R. L., & Weick, K. E. 1984. Toward a model of organizations as interpretation systems. ***Academy of Management Review,*** 9(2): 284-295.

Danneels, E. 2010. Trying to become a different type of company: dynamic capability at Smith Corona. ***Strategic Management Journal***, 32(1): 1-31.

Danneels, E. 2008. Organizational antecedents of second-order competences. ***Strategic Management Journal***, 29(5): 519-543.

Danneels, E. 2002. The dynamics of product innovation and firm competences. **Strategic Management Journal**, 23(12): 1095-1121

D'Aunno, T., Sutton, R. I., & Price, R. H. 1991. Isomorphism and external support in conflicting institutional environments: A study of drug abuse treatment units. ***Academy of Management Journal***, 34(3): 636-661.

D'Aveni, R. A. 1994. ***Hypercompetition: Managing the dynamics of strategic management***. New York.

D'Aveni, R. A., Dagnino, G. B., & Smith, K. G. 2010. The age of temporary advantage. ***Strategic Management Journal***, 31(13): 1371-1385.

Davis, J. P., & Eisenhardt, K. M., & Bingham, C. B. 2009. Optimal structure, market dynamism, and the strategy of simple rules. ***Administrative Science Quarterly***, 54(3): 413-452.

Day, D. V., & Lord, R. G. 1988. Executive leadership and organizational performance: Suggestions for a new theory and methodology. ***Journal of Management***, 14(3): 453-464.

Day, G. S., & Wensley, R. 1983. Marketing theory with a strategic orientation. ***The Journal of Marketing***, 47(4): 79-89.

De Jong, M. G., & Steenkamp, J. E. M., & Fox, J. 2007. Relaxing measurement invariance in cross-national consumer research using a hierarchical IRT model. ***Journal of Consumer Research***, 34(2): 260-278.

Denrell, J. 2002. The Intelligence of Superstition. ***Institute of International Business Stockholm School of Economics, Working Paper***, January.

Denrell, J. 2004. Random walks and sustained competitive advantage. ***Management Science***, 50(7): 922-934.

Derfus, P. J., Maggitti, P. G., Grimm, C. M., & Smith, K. G. 2008. The Red Queen effect: Competitive actions and firm performance. ***Academy of Management Journal***, 51(1): 61-80.

Diamantopoulos, A., & Winklhofer, H. M. 2001. Index construction with formative indicators: An alternative to scale development. ***Journal of Marketing Research***, 38(2): 269-277.

Dierickx, I., & Cool, K. 1989. Asset stock accumulation and sustainability of competitive advantage. ***Management Science***, 35(12): 1504-1511.

Di Stefano, G., Peteraf, M., & Verona, G. 2010. Dynamic capabilities deconstructed: A bibliographic investigation into the origins, development, and future directions of the research domain. ***Industrial and Corporate Change***, 19: 1187-1204.

Di Stefano, G., Peteraf, M., & Verona, G. 2014a. The organizational drivetrain: A road to integration of dynamic capabilities research. ***The Academy of Management Perspectives***, 28(4): 307-327.

Di Stefano, G., Peteraf, M., & Verona, G. 2014b. The elephant in the room of dynamic capabilities: Bringing two diverging conversations together. ***Strategic Management Journal***, 34(12): 1389-1410.

Døving, E., & Gooderham, P. N. 2008. Dynamic capabilities as antecedents of the scope of related diversification: the case of small firm accountancy practices. ***Strategic Management Journal***, 29(8): 841-857.

Dowling, M., & Helm, R. 2006. Product development success through cooperation: a study of entrepreneurial firms. ***Technovation***, 26(4): 483-488.

Drnevich, P. L., & Kriauciunas, A. P. 2011. Clarifying the conditions and limits of the contributions of ordinary and dynamic capabilities to relative firm performance. ***Strategic Management Journal***, 32(3): 254-279.

Dutton, J. E. 1992. The making of organizational opportunities: an interpretive pathway to organizational change. ***Research in Organizational Behavior***, 15: 195-226.

Dutton, J. E., & Duncan, R. B. 1987. The influence of the strategic planning process on strategic change. ***Strategic Management Journal***, 8(2): 103-116.

Dutton, J. E., Fahey, L., & Narayanan, U. K. 1983. Toward understanding strategic issue diagnosis. ***Strategic Management Joumal***, 4(4): 307-323.

Dutton, J. E., & Jackson, S. E. 1987. Categorizing strategic issues: Links to organizational actions. ***Academy of Management Review***, 12(1): 76-90.

Dutton, J. E., Stumpf, S. A., & Wagner, D. 1990. Diagnosing strategic issues and managerial investment of resources. In Shrivastav, P. and Lamb, R. B. (Eds), ***Advances in Strategic Management***. Greenwich, CT: JAI Press, 6: 143-67.

Easterby-Smith, M., Lyles, M. A., & Peteraf, M. A. 2009. Dynamic Capabilities: Current Debates and Future Directions. ***British Journal of Management***, 20(S1): 1-8.

Eberl, M. 2004. ***Formative und reflektive Indikatoren im Forschungsprozess, Schriften zur Empirischen Forschung und Quantitativen Unternehmensplanung***, Ludwig-Maximilians-Universität, München.

Edelman, M. 1977. ***Political Language.*** New York: Academic Press.

Eisenhardt, K. M. 1989. Making fast strategic decisions in high-velocity environments. ***Academy of Management Journal***, 32(3): 543-576.

Eisenhardt, K. M., & Martin, J. A. 2000. Dynamic capabilities: What are they? ***Strategic Management Journal***, 21(1): 1105-1121.

Ellonen, H. K., Wikström, P., & Jantunen, A. 2009. Linking dynamic-capability portfolios and innovation outcomes. ***Technovation***, 29(11): 753-762.

Eriksson, T. 2014. Processes, antecedents and outcomes of dynamic capabilities. ***Scandinavian Journal of Management***, 30(1): 65-82.

Ettlie, J. E., & Pavlou, P. A. 2006. Technology-based new product development partnerships. ***Decision Sciences***, 37(2): 117-147.

Fahey, L., & King, W. R. 1977. Environmental scanning for corporate planning. ***Business Horizons***, 20(4): 61-71.

Fang, E., & Zou, S. 2009. Antecedents and consequences of marketing dynamic capabilities in international joint ventures. ***Journal of International Business Studies***, 40(5): 742-761.

Farh, J. L., Hoffman, R. C., & Hegarty, W. H. 1984. Assessing environment scanning at the subunit level: A multitrait multimethod analysis. ***Decision Sciences***, 15(2): 197-220.

Fassott, G., & Eggert, A. 2005. Zur Verwendung formativer und reflektiver Indikatoren in Strukturgleichungsmodellen: Bestandsaufnahme und Anwendungsempfehlungen. ***Handbuch PLS-Pfadmodellierung: Methode, Anwendung, Praxisbeispiele***. Stuttgart: Schäffer-Poeschel.

Fey, C. F., & Birkinshaw, J. 2005. External sources of knowledge, governance mode, and R&D performance. ***Journal of Management***, 31(4): 597-621.

Fey, C. F., & Denison, D. R. 2003. Organizational culture and effectiveness: Can American theory be applied in Russia? ***Organization Science***, 14(6): 686-706.

Flores, L. G., Zheng, W., Rau, D., & Thomas, C. H. 2012. Organizational learning subprocess identification, construct validation, and an empirical test of cultural antecedents. ***Journal of Management***, 38(2): 640-667.

Ford, J. D., & Baucus, D. A. 1987. Organizational adaptation to performance downturns: An interpretation-based perspective. ***Academy of Management Review***, 12(2). 366-380.

Ford, J. K., MacCallum, R. C., & Tait, M. 1986. The application of exploratory factor analysis in applied psychology: A critical review and analysis. ***Personnel Psychology***, 39(2): 291-314.

Fornell, C., & Larcker, D. F. 1981. Evaluating structural equation models with unobservable variables and measurement error. ***Journal of Marketing Research***, 18(1): 39-50.

Fortune, A., & Mitchell, W. 2012. Unpacking Firm Exit at the Firm and Industry Levels: The Adaptation and Selection of Firm Capabilities. ***Strategic Management Journal***, 33(7): 794-819.

Foss, N. J. 1996. More Critical Comments on Knowledge-Based Theories of the Firm. ***Organization Science***, 7(5): 519–523.

Foss, N. J., Lyngsie, J., & Zahra, S. A. 2013. The role of external knowledge sources and organizational design in the process of opportunity exploitation. ***Strategic Management Journal***, 34(12): 1453-1471.

Fredrickson, J. W. 1985. Effects of decision motive and organizational performance level on strategic decision processes. ***Academy of Management Journal***, 28(4). 821-843.

Fuchs, C., & Diamantopoulos, A. 2009. Using single-item measures for construct measurement. ***Die Betriebswirtschaft***, 69(2): 195-210.

Galunic, D. C., & Eisenhardt, K. M. 2001. Architectural innovation and modular corporate forms. ***Academy of Management Journal***, 44(6): 1229-1249.

García-Morales, V. J., Llorens-Montes, F. J., & Verdu-Jover, A. J. 2007. Influence of personal mastery on organizational performance through organizational learning and innovation in large firms and SMEs. ***Technovation***, 27(9): 547-568.

Gerbing, D. W., & Anderson, J. C. 1988. An updated paradigm for scale development incorporating unidimensionality and its assessment. ***Journal of Marketing Research***, 25(2): 186-192.

Gilbert C. G. 2006. Change in the presence of residual fit: Can competing frames coexist? ***Organization Science,*** 17(1):150-167

Ginsberg, A. 1994. Minding the competition: From mapping to mastery. ***Strategic Management Journal***, 15(1): 153-174.

Ginsberg, A., & Venkatraman, N. 1995. Institutional initiatives for technological change: From issue interpretation to strategic choice. ***Organization Studies***, 16(3): 425-448.

Ginsberg, A. and Venkatraman, N. 1992. Investing in new information technology: the role of competitive posture and issue diagnosis. ***Strategic Management Journal***, 13(1): 37-53.

Gioia, D. A., Thomas, J. B., Clark, S. M. & Chittipeddi, K. 1994. Symbolism and strategic change in academia: the dynamics of sensemaking and influence. ***Organization Science***, 5(3): 363-383.

Goll, I., & Rasheed, A. 1997. Rational decision-making and firm performance: The moderating role of environment. ***Strategic Management Journal***, 18(7): 583-591.

Greenwood, R., & Hinings, C. R. 1996. Understanding radical organizational change: Bringing together the old and the new institutionalism. ***Academy of Management Review***, 21(4), 1022-1054.

Greenwood, P. E., & Nikolin, M. S. 1996. ***A guide to chi–squared testing***. New York: Wiley.

Hahn, E. D., & Doh, J. P. 2006. Using Bayesian methods in strategy research: an extension of Hansenet al. ***Strategic Management Journal***, 27(8): 783-798.

Hambrick, D. C. 1981. Environment, strategy, and power within top management teams. ***Administrative Science Quarterly***, 26(2): 253-275.

Hambrick, D. C. 1982. Environmental scanning and organizational strategy. ***Strategic Management Journal***, 3(2): 159-174.

Hambrick, D. C., & Mason, P. A. 1984. Upper echelons: The organization as a reflection of its top managers. ***Academy of Management Review***, 9(2): 193-206.

Hannan, M. T., & Freeman, J. H. 1977. The Population Ecology of Organizations. ***American Journal of Sociology***, 82(5): 929-964.

Hansen, M., Perry, L., & Reese, C. 2004. A Bayesian operationalization of the resource-based view. ***Strategic Management Journal***, 25(13): 1279-1295.

Harmancioglu, N., Grinstein, A., & Goldman, A. 2010. Innovation and performance outcomes of market information collection efforts: The role of top management team involvement. ***International Journal of Research in Marketing***, 27(1): 33-43.

Harreld, J. B., O'Reilly III, C. A., & Tushman, M. L. 2007. Driving strategy into action. ***California Management Review***, 49: 21-43.

Helfat, C. E. 1997. Know-how and asset complementarity and dynamic capability accumulation: The case of R&D. ***Strategic Management Journal***, 18(5): 339-360.

Helfat, C. E., Finkelstein, S., Mitchell, W., Peteraf, M., Singh, H., Teece, D., & Winter, S. G. 2007. ***Dynamic capabilities: Understanding strategic change in organizations.*** Malden, MA: Blackwell.

Helfat, C. E., & Peteraf, M. A. 2003. The dynamic resource-based view: Capability lifecycles. ***Strategic Management Journal***, 24(10): 997-1010.

Helfat, C. E., & Peteraf, M. A. 2009. Understanding dynamic capabilities: Progress along a developmental path. ***Strategic Organization***, 7(1): 91-102.

Helfat, C. E., & Peteraf, M. A. 2014. Managerial cognitive capabilities and the microfoundations of dynamic capabilities. ***Strategic Management Journal***. 36(6): 831-850.

Helfat, C. E., & Winter, S. G. 2011. Untangling dynamic and operational capabilities: Strategy for the (n)ever changing world. ***Strategic Management Journal***, 32(11): 1243-1250.

Helm, R., & Glück, T. 1997. Die Eignung verchiedener Pretests bei schriftlichen Befragungen. ***Jahrbuch der Absatz- und Verbrauchsforschung***, 43(3): 285-297.

Helm, R., & Gritsch, S. 2014. Examining the influence of uncertainty on marketing mix strategy elements in emerging business to business export-markets. ***International Business Review***, 23: 418-428.

Helm, R., Krinner, S., & Schmalfuß, M. 2014. Conceptualization and Integration of Marketing Intelligence: The Case of an Industrial Manufacturer. ***Journal of Business-to-Business Marketing***, 21: 237-255.

Helm, R., & Landschulze, S. 2013. How does consumer age affect the desire for new products and brands? A multi-group causal analysis. ***Review of Managerial Science***, 7: 29-59.

Henderson, R., & Mitchell, W. 1997. The interactions of organizational and competitive influences on strategy and performance. ***Strategic Management Journal***, 18(Summer Special Issue): 5-14.

Hennig-Thurau, T., & Dallwitz-Wegner, D. 2002. Online-Befragungen. Ein neues Instrument fur die Marktforschung. ***Wirtschaftswissenschaftliches Studium***, 31(6): 309-314.

Hills, G. E., & Shrader, R. C. 1998. Successful entrepreneurs' insights into opportunity recognition. ***Frontiers of Entrepreneurship Research***, 18: 30-41.

Hitt, M. A., Ireland, R. D., Camp, S. M., & Sexton, D. L. 2001. Strategic entrepreneurship: Entrepreneurial strategies for wealth creation. ***Strategic Management Journal***, 22(6-7): 479-491.

Hodgkinson, G. P. & Healey, M. P. 2011. Psychological foundations of dynamic capabilities: reflexion and reflection in strategic management. ***Strategic Management Journal***, 32(13): 1500-1516.

Hodgson, G. M. 1998. Evolutionary and Competence-based Theories of the Firm. ***Journal of Economic Studies,*** 25(1): 25-56.

Holland, W. E., Stead, B. A., & Leibrock, R. C. 1976. Information channel-source selection as a correlate of technical uncertainty in a research and development organization. ***IEEE Transactions on Engineering Management***, 23: 163-167.

House, R., Rousseau, D. M., & Thomas-Hunt, M. 1995. The meso paradigm: A framework for the integration of micro and macro organizational behavior. In L. L. Cummings & B. M. Staw (Eds.). ***Research in Organizational Behavior***, 17: 71-114. Greenwich, CT: JAI Press.

Howell, J. M., & Shea, C. M. 2001. Individual differences, environmental scanning, innovation framing, and champion behavior: key predictors of project performance. ***Journal of Product Innovation Management***, 18(1): 15-27.

Howell, J. M., Shea, C. M., & Higgins, C. A. 2005. Champions of product innovations: defining, developing, and validating a measure of champion behavior. ***Journal of BusinessVenturing***, 20: 641–661.

Hrebiniak, L. G., & Joyce, W. F. 1985. Organizational adaptation: Strategic choice and environmental determinism. ***Administrative Science Quarterly***, 30: 336-349.

Hu, L. T., & Bentler, P. M. 1999. Cutoff criteria for fit indexes in covariance structure analysis: Conventional criteria versus new alternatives. ***Structural Equation Modeling: A Multidisciplinary Journal***, 6(1): 1-55.

Huber, G. P. 1991. Organizational learning: The contributing processes and the literatures. ***Organization Science***, *2*(1): 88-115.

Huber, G. P., & Daft, R. L. 1987. The information environments of organizations. In Jablin, F., Putnam, L., Roberts, K. and Porter, L. (Eds.). ***Handbook of Organization Communication.*** Beverly Hills, CA: Sage, 130-164.

Hurmelinna-Laukkanen, P. 2012. Constituents and outcomes of absorptive capacity–appropriability regime changing the game. ***Management Decision***, 50(7): 1178-1199.

Hyland, P. W., Marceau, J., & Sloan, T. R. 2006. Sources of innovation and ideas in ICT firms in Australia. ***Creativity and Innovation Management***, 15 (2). 182-194.

Iansiti, M., & Clark, K. B. 1994. Integration and dynamic capability: Evidence from product development in automobiles and mainframe computers. ***Industrial and Corporate Change***, 3(3): 557-605.

Jackson, S. E. & Dutton, J. E. 1988. Discerning threats and opportunities. ***Administrative Science Quarterly***, 33(3): 370-87.

Jambulingam, T., Kathuria, R., & Doucette, W. R. 2005. Entrepreneurial orientation as a basis for classification within a service industry: The case of retail pharmacy industry. ***Journal of Operations Management***, 23(1): 23-42.

Jansen, J. J., Simsek, Z., & Cao, Q. 2012. Ambidexterity and performance in multiunit contexts: Cross level moderating effects of structural and resource attributes. ***Strategic Management Journal***, 33(11): 1286-1303.

Jarvis, C. B., MacKenzie, S. B., & Podsakoff, P. M. 2003. A critical review of construct indicators and measurement model misspecification in marketing and consumer research. ***Journal of Consumer Research***, 30(2): 199-218.

Jarzabkowski, P., Balogun, J., & Seidl, D. 2007. Strategizing: The challenges of a practice perspective. ***Human Relations***, 60(1): 5-27.

Jaworski, B. J., & Kohli, A. K. 1993. Market orientation: Antecedents and consequences. ***The Journal of Marketing***, 57(3): 53-70.

Jennings, D., & Jones, A. 1999. Environmental scanning in an emerging industry. ***Strategic Change***, 8(3): 153-162.

Johnson, G. L., Melin, L., & Whittington, R. 2003. Micro-strategy and strategizing. ***Journal of Management Studies***, 40: 3-22.

Jöreskog, K. G., & Sörbom, D. 1993. ***Lisrel 8: Structural equation modeling with the simplis command language***. Chicago, IL: Scientific Software International Inc.

Judge, W. Q., & Miller, A. 1991. Antecedents and outcomes of decision speed in different environmental contexts. ***Academy of Management Journal***, 34(2): 449-463.

Jung-Erceg, P., Pandza, K., Armbruster, H., & Dreher, C. 2007. Absorptive capacity in European manufacturing: A Delphi study. ***Industrial Management & Data Systems***, 107(1): 37-51.

Kahneman, D., & Tversky, A. 1979. Prospect theory: An analysis of decision under risk. ***Econometrica: Journal of the Econometric Society***, 47(2): 263-291.

Kale, P., & Singh, H. 2007. Building firm capabilities through learning: the role of the alliance learning process in alliance capability and firm- level alliance success. ***Strategic Management Journal***, 28(10): 981-1000.

Karim, S. 2006. Modularity in organizational structure: the reconfiguration of internally developed and acquired business units. ***Strategic Management Journal***, 27: 799-823.

Kerlinger, F. N. 1979. ***Behavioral research: A conceptual approach***. Harcourt School.

Kieser, A, & Ebers, M. 2006. ***Organisationstheorien***. Stuttgart: W. Kohlhammer Verlag.

Kiesler, S., & Sproull, L. 1982. Managerial response to changing environments: Perspectives on problem sensing from social cognition. ***Administrative Science Quarterly***, 27(4): 548-570.

Kindström, D., Kowalkowski, C., & Sandberg, E. 2012. Enabling service innovation: A dynamic capabilities approach. ***Journal of Business Research***, 66(8): 1063-1073.

King, A. A., & Tucci, C. L. 2002. Incumbent entry into new market niches: The role of experience and managerial choice in the creation of dynamic capabilities. ***Management Science***, 48(2): 171-186.

Kirzner, I. 1973. ***Competition and Entrepreneurship***. Chicago, IL: University of Chicago Press.

Kogut, B., & Zander, U. 1992. Knowledge of the firm, combinative capabilities, and the replication of technology. ***Organization Science***, 3(3): 383-397.

Kohli, A. K., Jaworski, B. J., & Kumar, A. 1993. MARKOR: A measure of market orientation. ***Journal of Marketing Research***, 30(4): 467-477.

Kohli, A. K., & Jaworski, B. J. 1990. Market orientation: The construct, research propositions, and managerial implications. ***The Journal of Marketing***, 54(2): 1-18.

Koppes, L. L., & Billings, R. S. 1988. A schematic perspective on problem identification. In Cardy, R. L., Puffer, S. M. and Newman, J. M. (Eds), ***Advances in Information Processing in Organizations.*** Greenwich, CT: JAI Press, 155-168.

Kor, Y. Y., & Leblebici, H. 2005. How do interdependencies among human-capital deployment, development, and diversification strategies affect firms' financial performance? ***Strategic Management Journal***, 26(10): 967-985.

Kor, Y. Y., & Mahoney, J. T. 2005. How dynamics, management, and governance of resource deployments influence firm- level performance. ***Strategic Management Journal***, 26(5): 489-496.

Kotler, P., Rackham, N., & Krishnaswamy, S. 2006. Ending the war between Sales & Marketing. ***Harvard Business Review,*** 84(7/8): 68-78.

Kraaijenbrink, J., Spender, J. C., & Groen, A. J. 2010. The resource-based view: a review and assessment of its critiques. ***Journal of Management***, 36(1): 349-372.

Kraatz, M. S., & Zajac, E. J. 2001. How organizational resources affect strategic change and performance in turbulent environments; theory and evidence. ***Organization Science***, 12(5): 632-657.

Kriz, A., Voola, R., & Yuksel, U. 2014. The dynamic capability of ambidexterity in hypercompetition: qualitative insights. ***Journal of Strategic Management***, 22(4): 287-299.

Krzakiewicz, K., & Cyfert, S. 2014. The Strategic Dimension of the Dynamic Capabilities of Enterprises. ***Management***, 18(2): 7-18.

Kuvaas, B. 2002. An exploration of two competing perspectives on informational contexts in top management strategic issue interpretation. ***Journal of Management Studies***, 39(7): 979-1003.

Lampel, J., & Shamsie, J. 2003. Capabilities in Motion: New Organizational Forms and the Reshaping of the Hollywood Movie Industry. ***Journal of Management Studies***, 40(8): 2189-2210.

Lavie, D. 2006. Capability reconfiguration: An analysis of incumbent responses to technological change. ***Academy of Management Review***, 31(1): 153-174.

Le Bon, J., & Merunka, D. 2006. The impact of individual and managerial factors on sales-people's contribution to marketing intelligence activities. ***International Journal of Research in Marketing***, 23(4): 395-408.

Lee, J., Lee, K., & Rho, S. 2002. An evolutionary perspective on strategic group emergence: a genetic algorithm- based model. ***Strategic Management Journal***, 23(8): 727-746.

Le Meunier-FitzHugh, K., & N. F. Piercy 2006. Integrating marketing intelligence sources. ***International Journal of Market Research***, 48(6): 699-716.

Lewin, A. Y. & Volberda, H. W. 1999. Prolegomena on coevolution: A framework for research on strategy and new organizational forms. ***Organization Science***, 10(5): 519-534

Li, D. Y., & Liu, J. 2014. Dynamic capabilities, environmental dynamism, and competitive advantage: Evidence from China. ***Journal of Business Research***, 67(1): 2793-2799.

Liao, J., Kickul, J. R., & Ma, H. 2009. Organizational Dynamic Capability and Innovation: An Empirical Examination of Internet Firms. ***Journal of Small Business Management***, 47(3): 263-286.

Lin, C. P., & Bhattacherjee, A. 2009. Understanding online social support and its antecedents: A socio-cognitive model. ***Social Science Journal***, 46(4): 724-737.

Lin, Y., & Wu, L. Y. 2014. Exploring the role of dynamic capabilities in firm performance under the resource-based view framework. ***Journal of Business Research***, 67(3): 407-413.

Lockett, A., Thompson, S., & Morgenstern, U. 2009. The development of the resource- based view of the firm: A critical appraisal. ***International Journal of Management Reviews***, 11(1): 9-28.

Lorenzoni, G., & Lipparini, A. 1999. The leveraging of interfirm relationships as a distinctive organizational capability: A longitudinal study. ***Strategic Management Journal***, 20(4): 317-338.

Lubit, R. 2001. Tacit Knowledge and Knowledge Management: The Keys to Sustainable Competitive Advantage. ***Organizational Dynamics,*** 29(4): 164-178.

Lukas, B. A., & Ferrell, O. C. 2000. The effect of market orientation on product innovation. ***Journal of the Academy of Marketing Science***, 28(2): 239-247.

Lumpkin, G. T., & Dess, G. G. 2006. The Effect of 'Simplicity'on the Strategy–Performance Relationship: A Note. ***Journal of Management Studies***, 43(7): 1583-1604.

Macher, J. T., & Mowery, D. C. 2009. Measuring Dynamic Capabilities: Practices and Performance in Semiconductor Manufacturing. ***British Journal of Management***, 20(S1): 41-62.

MacKenzie, S. B., Podsakoff, P. M., & Podsakoff, N. P. 2011. Construct measurement and validation procedures in MIS and behavioral research: Integrating new and existing techniques. ***MIS Quarterly***, 35(2): 293-334.

MacMillan, I. C. 1989. Delineating a forum for business policy scholars. ***Strategic Management Journal***, 10(4): 391 – 395.

Maier, J. L., Rainer Jr, R. K., & Snyder, C. A. 1997. Environmental scanning for information technology: An empirical investigation. ***Journal of Management Information Systems***, 14(2): 177-200.

Mahoney, J., & Rueschemeyer, D. 2003. ***Comparative Historical Analysis in the Social Sciences***. Cambridge: Cambridge University Press.

Makadok, R. 2001. Toward a synthesis of the resource-based and dynamic-capability views of rent creation. **Strategic Management Journal**, 22(5): 387-401.

Malik, F., & Probst, G. 1981. Evolutionäres Management. ***Die Unternehmung***, 35(2), 121-140.

March 1994. The evolution of evolution. In Joel A. C. Baum, Jitendra V. Singh (Eds). ***Evolutionary Dynamics of Organizations***. New York: Oxford University Press: 39-49.

March, J. G., & Simon, H. A. 1958. ***Organizations.*** New York, London: Wiley.

Marcus, A. A., & Anderson, M. H. 2006. A General Dynamic Capability: Does it Propagate Business and Social Competencies in the Retail Food Industry?* ***Journal of Management Studies***, 43(1): 19-46.

Matsuno, K., Mentzer, J. T., & Rentz, J. O. 2000. A refinement and validation of the MARKOR scale. ***Journal of the Academy of Marketing Science***, 28(4): 527-539.

May, R. C., Stewart, W. H., & Sweo, R. 2000. Environmental scanning behavior in a transitional economy: Evidence from Russia. ***Academy of Management Journal***, 43(3): 403-427.

McKelvie, A., & Davidsson, P. 2009. From Resource Base to Dynamic Capabilities: an Investigation of New Firms. ***British Journal of Management***, 20(1): 63-80.

McNamara, G., Valler, P. M., & Devers, C. 2003. Same as it ever was: The search for evidence of increasing hypercompetition. ***Strategic Management Journal***, 24(3): 261-278.

Meyer, J. W., & Rowan, B. 1977. Institutionalized organizations: Formal structure as myth and ceremony. ***American Journal of Sociology***, 83(2): 340-363.

Meyer, J.W., Scott, W.R., Deal, T. 1979. Institutional and Technical Sources of Organizational Structure Explaining the Structure of Educational Organizations. ***Working Paper, Stanford University.***

Miles, R. E., & Snow, C. C. 1994. ***Fit, Failure, and the Hall of Fame: How Companies Succeed or Fail***. New York: Free Press.

Miller, D. 1990. ***The Icarus Paradox: How Exceptional Companies Bring about Their Own Downfall***. New York: Harper-Collins.

Miller, D., & Friesen, P. H. 1983. Strategy making and environment: The third link. ***Strategic Management Journal***, 4(3): 221-235.

Milliken, F. J. 1990. Perceiving and interpreting environmental change: An examination of college administrators' interpretation of changing demographics. ***Academy of Management Journal***, 33(1): 42-63.

Mintzberg, H. 1979. ***The structuring of organizations: A synthesis of the research***. University of Illinois at Urbana-Champaign's Academy for Entrepreneurial Leadership Historical Research Reference in Entrepreneurship.

Moliterno, T. P., & Wiersema, M. F. 2007. Firm performance, rent appropriation, and the strategic resource divestment capability. ***Strategic Management Journal***, 28(11): 1065-1087.

Möller, K., & Rajala, A. 2007. Rise of strategic nets—New modes of value creation. ***Industrial Marketing Management***, 36(7): 895-908.

Montgomery, D. B., Moore, M. C., & Urbany, J. E. 2005. Reasoning about competitive reactions: evidence from executives. ***Marketing Science***, 24(1): 138-49.

Nadler, D.A. 1998. ***Champions of Change***. San Francisco, CA: Jossey-Bass.

Narayanan, V. K., Colwell, K., & Douglas, F. L. 2009 Building Organizational and Scientific Platforms in the Pharmaceutical Industry: A Process Perspective on the Development of Dynamic Capabilities. ***British Journal of Management***, 20(1): 25-40.

Narver, J. C., & S. F. Slater 1990. The effect of a market orientation on business profitability. ***Journal of Marketing***, 54(5): 20-35.

Narver, J. C., Slater, S. F., & MacLachlan, D. L. 2004. Responsive and proactive market orientation and new product success. ***Journal of Product Innovation Management***, 21(5): 334-347.

Nastanski, M. 2004. The value of active scanning to senior executives: Insights from key decision-makers. ***Journal of Management Development***, 23(5): 426-436.

Nelson, R. R., & Winter, S. G. 1982, ***An Evolutionary Theory of Economic Change***. Cambridge, MA: Harvard University Press.

Netemeyer, R. G., Bearden, W. O., & Sharma, S. (Eds.). 2003. ***Scaling procedures: Issues and applications***. Palo Alto, CA: Sage Publications.

Newe, L. R., & Zahra, S. A. 2009. The Evolving Firm: How Dynamic and Operating Capabilities Interact to Enable Entrepreneurship. ***British Journal of Management***, 20(S1): 81-100.

Ngo, L. V., & O'Cass, A. 2012. Performance implications of market orientation, marketing resources, and marketing capabilities. ***Journal of Marketing Management***, 28 (1/2): 173-187.

Nunnally, J. C., & Bernstein, I. H. 1994. ***Psychometric Theory***. New York: McGraw-Hill.

Ocasio, W. 1995. The enactment of economic adversity: A reconciliation of theories of failure-induced change and threat rigidity. In L. L. Cummings and B. M. Staw (Eds.) ***Research in Organizational Behavior***, 17. Greenwick, CT: JAI Press, 287-331.

Oliver, C., & Holzinger, I. 2008. The effectiveness of strategic political management: A dynamic capabilities framework. ***Academy of Management Review***, 33(2): 496-520.

O'Reilly, C. A. 1982. Variations in decision makers' use of information sources: the impact of quality and accessibility of information. ***Academy of Management Journal***, 25(4): 756-771.

Pablo, A. L., Reay, T., Dewald, J. R., & Casebeer, A. L. 2007. Identifying, enabling and managing dynamic capabilities in the public sector. ***Journal of Management Studies***, 44(5): 687-708.

Paternoster, R., Brame, R., Mazerolle, P., & Piquero, A. 1998. Using the correct statistical test for the equality of regression coefficients. ***Criminology***, 36(4): 859-866.

Pavlou, P. A., & El Sawy, O. A. 2006. From IT leveraging competence to competitive advantage in turbulent environments: The case of new product development. ***Information Systems Research***, 17(3): 198-227.

Pavlou, P. A., & El Sawy, O. A. 2011. Understanding the elusive black box of dynamic capabilities. ***Decision Sciences***, 42(1): 239-273.

Penrose, E. T. 1959. ***The Theory of the Growth of the Firm.*** New York: Wiley.

Penrose, E. T. 2009. ***The Theory of the Growth of the Firm***. Oxford: Oxford University Press.

Pettigrew, A., & Whip, R. 1991. ***Managing Change for Competitive Success***, Oxford: Basil Blackwell.

Pfeffer, J., & Salancik, G. R. 1978. ***The external control of organizations: A resource dependence approach.*** New York: Harper and Row Publishers.

Phelan, S. E., & Lewin, P. 2000. Arriving at a strategic theory of the firm. ***International Journal of Management Reviews***, 2(4): 305-323.

Pil, F. K., & Cohen, S. K. 2006. Modularity: implications for imitation, innovation, and sustained advantage. ***Academy of Management Review***, 31(4): 995-1011.

Podsakoff, P. M., & Organ, D. W. 1986. Self-reports in organizational research: Problems and prospects. ***Journal of Management***, 12(4): 69-82.

Podsakoff, P. M., MacKenzie, S. B., Lee, J. Y., & Podsakoff, N. P. 2003. Common method biases in behavioral research: A critical review of the literature and recommended remedies. ***Journal of Applied Psychology***, 88(5): 879-903.

Porter, M. E. 1980. ***Competitive Strategy***. New York: Free Press

Porter, M. E. 1985. Technology and competitive advantage. ***Journal of Business Strategy***, 5(3): 60-78.

Prahalad, C. K., & Hamel, G. 1990. The core competence of the corporation. ***Harvard Business Review***, 68(3), 79-91.

Prieto, I. M., Revilla, E., & Rodriguez-Prado, B. 2009. Building dynamic capabilities in product development: How do contextual antecedents matter? ***Scandinavian Journal of Management***, 25(3): 313-326.

Probst, G. J. 1987. Selbstorganisation und Entwicklung. ***Die Unternehmung***, 41(4) 242-255.

Protogerou, A., Caloghirou, Y., & Lioukas, S. 2012. Dynamic capabilities and their indirect impact on firm performance. ***Industrial and Corporate Change***, 21(3): 615-647.

Ramón Oreja-Rodríguez, J., & Yanes-Estévez, V. 2010. Environmental scanning: dynamism with rack and stack from Rasch model. ***Management Decision***, 48(2): 260-276.

Reeves, M., & Deimler, M. 2011. Adaptability: The New Competitive Advantage. ***Harvard Business Review,*** July-August: 134-141.

Reilly, M., & Sharkey Scott, P. 2010. Dynamic Capabilities, Absorptive Capacity and Knowledge Sharing: A Research Agenda Into Explicating the Antecedent Factors Conducive to Subsidiary Bargaining Power. ***Academy of International Business*** (UKI Chapter), Conference Paper, Trinity College Dublin.

Richard, P. J., Devinney, T. M., Yip, G. S., & Johnson, G. 2009. Measuring organizational performance: Towards methodological best practice. ***Journal of Management***, 35: 718-804.

Rindova, V. P., & Kotha, S. 2001. Continuous "morphing": Competing through dynamic capabilities, form, and function. ***Academy of Management Journal***, 44(6): 1263-1280.

Robinson, S., & Stubberud, H. A. 2011. Sources of information and cooperation for innovation in Norway. ***Journal of International Business Research***, 10(2): 91-102.

Rosenbloom, R. S. 2000. Leadership, capabilities, and technological change: The transformation of NCR in the electronic era. ***Strategic Management Journal***, 21(10-11): 1083-1103.

Rosenkopf, L., & Nerkar, A. 2001. Beyond local search: Boundary spanning, exploration, and impact in the optical disk industry. ***Strategic Management Journal***, 22(4): 287-306.

Rossiter, J. R. 2002. The C-OAR-SE procedure for scale development in marketing. ***International Journal of Research in Marketing***, 19(4), 305-335.

Rothaermel, F. T., & Hess, A. M. 2007. Building dynamic capabilities: Innovation driven by individual-, firm-, and network-level effects. ***Organization Science***, 18(6): 898-921.

Rubin, D. B. 1973. The use of matched sampling and regression adjustment to remove bias in observational studies. ***Biometrics***, 29(1): 185-203.

Ruefli, R. W., Collins, J. M., & Lacugna, J. R. 1999. Risk measures in strategic management research: Auld lang syne? ***Strategic Management Journal***, 20(2): 167- 194.

Rumelt, R. P. 1974. ***Strategy, structure, and economic performance***. Cambridge, MA: Harvard University Press.

Salvato, C. 2003. The Role of Micro- Strategies in the Engineering of Firm Evolution. ***Journal of Management Studies***, 40(1): 83-108.

Schilke, O. 2014. Second-order dynamic capabilities; how do they matter? ***Academy of Management Perspectives***, 28(4): 368-380.

Schilke, O., 2013. On the contingent value of dynamic capabilities for competitive advantage: The nonlinear moderating effect of environmental dynamism. ***Strategic Management Journal***, 35(2): 179-203.

Schnell, R., Hill, P. B., & Esser, E. 2008. ***Methoden der empirischen Sozialforschung.*** München: Oldenburg Verlag.

Schreyögg, G., & Kliesch-Eberl, M. 2007. How dynamic can organizational capabilities be? Towards a dual-process model of capability dynamization. ***Strategic Management Journal***, 28(9): 913-933.

Schumpeter, J. A. 1934. ***The theory of economic development: An inquiry into profits, capital, credit, interest, and the business cycle.*** New Brunswick, NJ: Transaction publishers.

Scott, W. R. 1987. The adolescence of institutional theory. ***Administrative Science Quarterly***, 32(4): 493-511.

Senge, P. M. 1990. ***The fifth discipline: The art and practice of the learning organization***. New York: Broadway Business.

Severi Bruni, D., & Verona, G. 2009. Dynamic Marketing Capabilities in Science-based Firms: an Exploratory Investigation of the Pharmaceutical Industry. ***British Journal of Management***, 20(1): 101-117.

Sharma, S., Mukherjee, S., Kumar, A. & Dillon, W. R. 2005. A simulation study to investigate the use of cutoff values for assessing model fit in covariance structure models. ***Journal of Business Research***, 58(7): 935-943.

Sharma, S. 2000. Managerial interpretations and organizational context as predictors of corporate choice of environmental strategy. ***Academy of Management Journal***, 43(4): 681-697.

Shimizu, K. 2007. Prospect Theory, Behavioral Theory, and the Threat-rigidity Thesis: Combinative Effects on Organizational Decisions to Divest Formerly Acquired Units. ***Academy of Management Journal,*** 50(6): 1495-1514.

Shook, C. L., Ketchen, D. J., Hult, G. T. M., & Kacmar, K. M. 2004. An assessment of the use of structural equation modeling in strategic management reseearch. ***Strategic Management Journal***, 25(4): 397-404.

Simon, H. A. 1955. A behavioral model of rational choice. ***The Quarterly Journal of Economics***, 69(1): 99-118.

Simon, H. A. 1976. ***Administrative Behavior. A Study of Decision-Making Processes in Administrative Organizations.*** New York: Free Press.

Simon, H. A. 1991. Bounded rationality and organizational learning. ***Organization Science***, 2:125-135.

Singh, R. P., Hills, G. E., Lumpkin, G. T., & Hybels, R. C. 1999. The entrepreneurial opportunity recognition process: examining the role of selfperceived alertness and social networks. ***Academy of Management Proceedings***, G1-G6.

Sittimalakorn, W., & Hart, S. 2004. Market orientation versus quality orientation: sources of superior business performance. ***Journal of Strategic Marketing***, 12(4): 243-253.

Slater, S. F., Olson, E. M., & Hult, G. T. M. 2006. The moderating influence of strategic orientation on the strategy formation capability–performance relationship. ***Strategic Management Journal***, 27(12): 1221-1231.

Smith, K. G., Collins, C. J., & Clark, K. D. 2005. Existing knowledge, knowledge creation capability, and the rate of new product introduction in high-technology firms. ***Academy of Management Journal***, 48(2): 346-357.

Song, M., Droge, C., Hanvanich, S., & Calantone, R. 2005. Marketing and technology resource complementarity: An analysis of their interaction effect in two environmental contexts. ***Strategic Management Journal***, 26(3): 259-276.

Starbuck, W. H., & Milliken, F. J. 1988. Challenger: fine- tuning the odds until something breaks. ***Journal of Management Studies***, *25*(4): 319-340.

Stata, R. 1989. Organizational Learning: The Key to Market Innovation, ***Sloan Market Review***, 30: 63-74.

Staw, B. M., & Ross, J. 1978. Commitment to a policy decision: A multi-theoretical perspective. ***Administrative Science Quarterly***, 23(1): 40-64.

Staw, B. M., Sandelands, L. E., & Dutton, J. E. 1981. Threat rigidity effects in organizational behavior: A multilevel analysis. ***Administrative Science Quarterly***, 26(4): 501-524.

Sutcliffe, K. M. 1997. Commentary: Strategic sense-making: learning through scanning, interpretation, action, and performance. In Shrivastava, P., Huff, A. S. and Dutton, J. E. (Eds). ***Advances in Strategic Management***. Greenwich, CT: JAI Press, 14: 331-336.

Talke, K., & Colarelli O'Connor, G. 2011. Conveying effective message content when launching new industrial products. ***Journal of Product Innovation Management***, 28(6): 943-956.

Teece, D. J. 1982. Towards an economic theory of the multiproduct firm. ***Journal of Economic Behavior & Organization***, 3(1): 39-63.

Teece, D. J. 1986. Profiting from technological innovation: Implications for integration, collaboration, licensing and public policy. ***Research Policy***, 15(6): 285-305.

Teece, D. J. 1988. Capturing value from technological innovation: Integration, strategic partnering, and licensing decisions. ***Interfaces***, 18(3): 46-61.

Teece, D. J. 2007. Explicating dynamic capabilities: The nature and microfoundations of (sustainable) enterprise performance. ***Strategic Management Journal***, 28(13): 1319-1350.

Teece, D. J. 2012. Dynamic Capabilities: Routines versus Entrepreneurial Action. ***Journal of Management Studies***, 49(8): 1395-1401.

Teece, D. J., & Pisano, G. 1994. The dynamic capabilities of firms: An introduction. ***Industrial and Corporate Change***, 3(3): 537-556.

Teece, D. J., Pisano, G., & Shuen, A. 1997. Dynamic capabilities and strategic management. ***Strategic Management Journal***, 18(7): 509-533.

Teece, D. J., R. Rumelt, G. Dosi, & Winter, S. 1994. Understanding Corporate Coherence. Theory and Evidence. ***Journal of Economic Behavior and Organization***, 23: 1-30.

Thaler, R. H., & Johnson, E. J. 1990. Gambling with the house money and trying to break even: The effects of prior outcomes on risky choice. ***Management Science,*** 36(6): 643-660.

Thomas, J. B., Clark, S. M. & Gioia, D. A. 1993. Strategic sensemaking and organizational performance: Linkages among scanning, interpretation, action, and outcomes. ***Academy of Management Journal***, 36(2): 239-270.

Thomas, J. B., Gioia, D. A. & Ketchen, D. J. 1997. Strategic sense-making: learning through scanning, interpretation, action, and performance. In Shrivastava, P., Huff, A. S. and Dutton, J. E. (Eds). ***Advances in Strategic Management***. Greenwich, CT: JAI Press, 14: 299-329.

Townsend, D., & Busenitz, L. 2015. Turning water into wine? Exploring the role of dynamic capabilities in early-stage capitalization processes. ***Journal of Business Venturing***, 30(2): 292-306.

Tripsas, M., & Gavetti, G. 2000. Capabilities, cognition, and inertia: Evidence from digital imaging. ***Strategic Management Journal***, 21(10-11): 1147-1161.

Tseng, S. M., & Lee, P. S. 2014. The effect of knowledge management capability and dynamic capability on organizational performance. ***Journal of Enterprise Information Management***, 27(2): 158-179.

Tversky, A., & Kahneman, D. 1981. The framing of decisions and the psychology of choice. ***Science***, 211(4481): 453-458.

Tversky, A., & Kahneman, D. 1986. Rational choice and the framing of decisions. ***Journal of Business***, 59(4): 251-278.

Vandenbosch, B., Saatcioglu, A., & Fay, S. 2006. Idea management: a systemic view. ***Journal of Management Studies***, 43: 259-288.

Von den Driesch, T., da Costa, M. E. S., Flatten, T. C., & Brettel, M. 2015. How CEO experience, personality, and network affect firms' dynamic capabilities. ***European Management Journal***, in press.

Von der Lippe, P., & Kladroba, A. 2002. Repräsentativität von Stichproben. ***Marketing ZFP***, 24(2): 139-145.

Von Krogh, G., & Roos, J. 1996. ***Managing knowledge: Perspectives on cooperation and competition***. London: Sage Publications.

Wang, C. L., & Ahmed, P. A. 2007. Dynamic Capabilities: A Review and Research Agenda. ***International Journal of Management Reviews*** 9(1): 31-51.

Wang, Y. L., Ellinger, A. D., & Wu, Y. C. J. 2013. Entrepreneurial opportunity recognition: An empirical study of R&D personnel. ***Management Decision***, 51(2): 248 266.

Weber, W., & Kabst, R. 2004. Human resource management: the need for theory and diversity. ***Management Revue***, 15(2): 171-177.

Weiber, R., & Mühlhaus, D. 2010. ***Strukturgleichungsmodellierung***. Eine anwendungsorientierte Einführung in die Kausalanalyse mit Hilfe von AMOS, SmartPLS und SPSS. Heidelberg: Springer Verlag.

Wernerfelt, B. 1984. A resource- based view of the firm. ***Strategic Management Journal***, 5(2): 171-180.

Weston, R., & Gore Jr., P. A. 2006. A brief guide to structural equation modeling, ***The Counseling Psychologist***, 34(5): 719-751.

White, C. J., Varadarajan, P. R., & Dacin, P. A. 2003. Market situation interpretation and response: the role of cognitive style, organizational culture, and information use. ***Journal of Marketing***, 67 (3): 63-79.

Wiggins, R. R., & Ruefli, T. W. 2005. Schumpeter's ghost: Is hypercompetition making the best of times shorter? ***Strategic Management Journal***, 26(10): 887-911.

Wilden, R. & Gudergan, S. 2015. The impact of dynamic capabilities on operational marketing and technological capabilities: investigating the role of environmental turbulence. ***Journal of the Academy of Marketing Science***, 43(2): 181-199.

Wilden, R., Gudergan, S., Nielsen, B., & Lings, I. 2013. Dynamic Capabilities and Performance: Strategy, Structure and Environment. ***Long Range Planning***, 46(1-2): 72-96.

Wilhelm, H., Schlömer, M., & Maurer, I. 2015. How Dynamic Capabilities Affect the Effectiveness and Efficiency of Operating Routines under High and Low Levels of Environmental Dynamism. ***British Journal of Management***, 26(2): 327-345.

Williamson, O. E. 1975. ***Markets and Hierarchies.*** New York: The Free Press.

Williamson, O. E. 1985. ***The Economic Institutions of Capitalism***. New York: The Free Press.

Winter, S. G. 1987. Knowledge and Competence as Strategic Assets. In D. J. Teece (Eds.) ***The Competitive Challenge: Strategies for Industrial Innovation and Renewal.*** Cambridge, MA: Ballinger, 159–184.

Winter, S. G. 2003. Understanding dynamic capabilities. ***Strategic Management Journal***, 24(10): 991-995.

Wold, H. 1966. Nonlinear estimation by partial least squares procedures. In David, F. N. (Eds.) ***Research papers in statistics***. New York: Wiley, 411- 444.

Wold, H. 1980. Model Construction and Evaluation when Theoretical Knowledge is Scarce. In Kmenta, J. & Ramsey, J. B. (Eds.) ***Evaluation of Econometric Models***, New York: Wiley, 47-74.

Wold, H. 1982. Soft Modeling: The Basic Design and Some Extensions. In Jöreskog, K. G. & Wold, H. (Eds.) ***Systems under indirect Observation, Part II***, 138: 1-54.

Wu, L. 2007. Entrepreneurial resources, dynamic capabilities and start-up performance of Taiwan's high-tech firms. ***Journal of Business Research***, 60(5): 549-555.

Yang, C., & Liu, H. M. 2012. Boosting firm performance via enterprise agility and network structure. ***Management Decision***, 50(6): 1022-1044.

Yi, Y., He, X., Ndofor, H. & Wie, Z. 2015. Dynamic capabilities and the Speed of Strategic Change: Evidence From China. ***IEEE Transactions on Engineering Management***, 62(1): 18-28.

Yin, R. K. 2014. ***Case study research: Design and methods***. Thousand Oaks, CA: Sage Publications.

Young, G., Smith, K. G., & Grimm, C. M. 1996. "Austrian" and industrial organization perspectives on firm-level competitive activity and performance. ***Organization Science***, 7(3): 243-254.

Zahra, S. A., & Nielsen, A. P. 2002. Sources of capabilities, integration and technology commercialization. ***Strategic Management Journal***, 23(5): 377-398.

Zahra, S. A., Sapienza, H. J., & Davidsson, P. 2006. Entrepreneurship and dynamic capabilities: a review, model and research agenda. ***Journal of Management Studies***, 43(4): 917-955.

Zhang, M. J. 2007. IS support for top managers' dynamic capabilities, environmental dynamism, and firm performance: An empirical investigation. ***Journal of Business & Management***, 13(1): 57-77.

Zollo, M., & Winter, S. G. 2002. Deliberate learning and the evolution of dynamic capabilities. ***Organization Science***, 13(3): 339-351.

Zott, C. 2003. Dynamic capabilities and the emergence of intraindustry differential firm performance: insights from a simulation study. ***Strategic Management Journal***, 24(2): 97-125.

Zúñiga- Vicente, J. Á., & Vicente- Lorente, J. D. 2006. Strategic Moves and Organizational Survival in Turbulent Environments: The Case of Spanish Banks (1983–97). ***Journal of Management Studies***, 43(3): 485-519.